the magic of
Crazy Quilting
SECOND EDITION

A Complete Resource for Embellished Quilting

J. Marsha Michler

Published by

krause publications
An F&W Publications Company

700 East State Street • Iola, WI 54990-0001
715-445-2214 • 888-457-2873
www.krause.com

To place an order or obtain a free catalog, please call 800-258-0929.

Library of Congress Catalog Number 98-84098
ISBN 0-87349-724-4

The following registered trademark terms and companies appear in this publication:
Silk Serica® is a registered trademark of **Kreinik Mfg. Co. Inc**.
DMC® is a registered trademark of the **DMC Corporation**.
Paternayan® is a registered trademark of **JCA, Inc**.
Impressions®, Wildflowers®, Waterlilies®, are registered trademarks of **The Caron Collection**.
Piecemakers® is a registered trademark of **Piecemakers Country Store**.
Pentel® is a registered trademark of the **Pentel Co., Ltd**.
Apple Barrel Colors®, and Plaid® are registered trademarks of **Plaid Enterprises, Inc**.

Edited by Christine Townsend
Designed by Donna Mummery
Photography by J. Marsha Michler and Robert Best

Printed in the United States of America

Frontpiece from an 1800's book.

Dedication

For my son, Ben.

Acknowledgments

My most heartfelt thanks to those who contributed in so many ways to this book. Thanks to the folks at Krause for allowing this new edition to happen including Julie Stephani, Christine Townsend, editor; Donna Mummery , book designer. To the original editors, Gabrielle Wyant-Perillo and Kris Manty, and designer, Jan Wojtech: I still say "thanks." Then as now, I want to thank Joe Hudgins for sharing his knowledge of cigarette silks, Diana Vandervoort for her gracious encouragement, Cindy Smith of the Limerick Public Library for her research assistance, Paula Robert of Copy-It in Biddeford Maine, Jeanette Brewster of the Valley Needlers Quilt Guild.

Many thanks to those who contributed in many ways including supplies, photographs, and information: Kim Kovaly, Maggie Backman of Things Japanese, Anna Baird, Nancy Kirk of the Kirk Collection, Dena Lenham of Kreinik Mfg. Co. Inc., Elda O'Connell, Catherine Carpenter, Mary Weinberg.

Those who graciously assisted in my study of crazy quilts include Betsey Telford of Rocky Mountain Quilts in York Village, Maine; Richard T. Eisenhower, Marcene J. Modeland, and Pamela S. Eagleson of The Brick Store Museum in Kennebunk, Maine; Joan Sylvester of the Shiretown Antique Center; Bonnie Hayward of Avalon Antiques; The Gold Bug Antiques of Cape Neddick, Maine; The Barn at Cape Neddick, Maine; Tina Toomey of the York Institute Museum in Saco Maine; and the Maine Historical Society in Portland, Maine.

Thanks to Dover Publications, Inc. for granting permission to use Victorian clip art from the books: Victorian Frames, Borders, and Cuts; Victorian Pictorial Borders, Borders, Frames and Decorative Motifs from the 1862 Derriey Typographic Catalog; Treasury of Victorian Printers' Frames, Ornaments and Initials; and Victorian Spot Illustrations, Alphabets and Ornaments.

And, my thanks, deepest appreciation, and admiration to Limerick's very special "quilters" who are Kim and Lauren Kovaly, Marian Budzyna, Jane Bryant, Kathy Melzer, Adele and Ruth Floyd, Paul Baresel, and Peg Gomane.

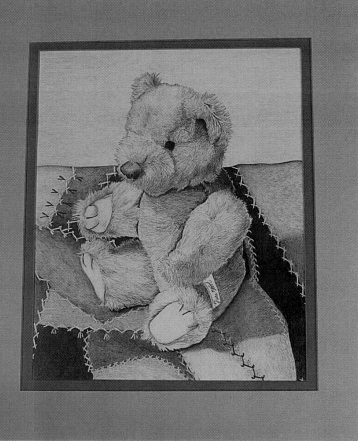

Teddy bear on a crazy quilt. Pencil drawing by the author.

Contents

Introduction

The years marked by Queen Victoria's reign, 1838 to 1901, were characterized by massive and significant social changes. The romance in the age is in the phenomenal opening of trade, the boom in technology, and the emergence of entrepreneurial business ventures. The "Iron Horse" began to course its way across entire continents. Toilets became flushable, silks became available and affordable, and telegraph cables literally connected continents. Electricity made lighting a home easy, and medical advances saved lives. The color mauve was discovered, the sewing machine was invented, and the search was on for a synthetic silk. With industry, art was undergoing major changes. Painters studied the science of light and color. They began juxtaposing colors in ways that the eye would mix them. Artists such as Monet sought to capture the effects of light, while Seurat created paintings entirely of dots. These and other artists were the vanguard of the modern art movement. They were very different from the prior academic style with its realism and layer upon layer of well-oiled paint.

Victorian-age needlework was rich and varied. It is fitting that women, reacting to the changes around them, attempted unconventional forms in their quilting. The play of colors and textures placed on a quilt top, and united with embroidery stitches, are every bit as artistic as the works of the painters. Some crazy quilts of late Victorian times display a range of highly developed needlework skills, combined with a refined sense of color and composition. These quilts often feature ribbon work, ribbon embroidery, monogramming, embroidery stitches of all types and other forms of needlework. At times they included paintings on fabric in a complex mix of ingredients.

There is no identifiable "inventor" of the crazy quilt. It seems to have been congruous with the era in which it was born—but, like fads that occur today, crazy quilting gained rapid momentum. It appears to have originated in America, and gained steam from about 1860. The phase culminated around the 1880s and fizzled out in the early 1900s. The appeal of crazy quilting to Victorian ladies must have subsequently inspired the rage. These ladies adored them the same as we do today—seeking out a wonderful collection of "finds," fancy fabrics, and luxurious threads, and then assembling them into a showpiece quilt.

About Crazy Quilting

Crazy quilting is the placing together of irregular-shaped patches, usually onto a foundation, after which they are usually secured with embroidery stitches. Often used are fancy fabrics from dressmaking, draperies, bridal apparel, and other fancy additions. A wide variety of embellishments and embroidery stitches added to the patches dramatically bring the patched surface to life.

The true magic of crazy quilting is in the melding of its ingredients and the individuality of each hand's work. There is a magical transformation that takes place with the laying of patches and the addition of embroidery stitches and embellishments. You never truly know what a quilt or project is going to look like until the final stitches are placed.

The word "crazy" beautifully sums up what is unique about this type of quilting. It is perfect if you feel a little bit crazy while working on your crazy quilt! This is a form of quilting that utilizes your most pure imaginativeness from beginning to end. For those who make these quilts, the joy of creativity truly blossoms.

How to Use This Book

Read this book from front to back, or use it as a reference volume. I recommend that beginners read it through to become familiar with the basic procedures and the many options. More experienced workers may prefer to reference individual topics.

I present *The Magic of Crazy Quilting* with the crazy quilt in mind. However, the techniques and embroidery stitches throughout the book apply to a variety of quilt types and many needlework projects.

Chapter 1

The Basics of Crazy Quilting

Simple Requirements

Here are the essential tools for crazy quilting. Additional requirements for different methods and embellishments are covered under the individual topics. When purchasing tools, buy the highest quality. You will find that quality does make a difference.

Shears and Scissors

Have a good, 7" or 8" fabric shears that cuts fabric effortlessly, and use it only for cutting fabric. These come with plastic handles, but I prefer the all-metal variety. A good pair of all-metal shears seems expensive, but the initial cost pays off in ease of handling and maneuverability.

Embroidery scissors come in a variety of styles and sizes. Again, I prefer the all-metal kinds that have a wide blade and a narrow one. These are not only for cutting threads, but can also be used for trimming and for cutting small pieces of fabrics.

For traveling, carry inexpensive thread clippers instead of good scissors. Like pens, scissors are often borrowed, and they can slip out of your bag.

Add a paper cutting scissors to your tool collection for cutting out paper patterns and tissue paper. Cutting paper dulls the blades of your good shears and scissors.

Needles and Pins

Three types of handsewing needles will accommodate almost any technique in crazy quilting: embroidery/crewel, chenille, and appliqué/size 12 sharps. Purchase assorted sizes of the embroidery and chenille needles, for use with a variety of threads and ribbons.

The needle's purpose is to make a large enough hole in the fabric for the thread or ribbon to slide through effortlessly. At the same time, it should hold the thread snug enough so it doesn't fall out of the needle's eye.

Although they slip through and stick fingers, evade grasp, and often become stuck in the carpet, pins are among the most useful tools for crazy quilting. I use silk pins for almost everything—they create fewer bulges in the fabric, and pressing is easier with the smaller heads. If using pins with beaded heads, choose those with glass beads, which will not melt under the iron.

Embroidery Hoops

A 4" hoop is excellent for doing small areas of ribbon embroidery, beadwork, and punchneedle. Use a larger hoop (6" or more) for embroidery along patch seams.

**A good scissors to treasure,
Is both delight and pleasure.
But in public is not to share—
Too likely to dis-a-pair!**

Only a few tools are required for crazy quilting. Some antique tools are still useful today, such as this pin-cushion/ thread stand.

Hold a laying tool in one hand, while using the needle in the other. The quilt is in a lap hoop.

If your patch fabrics and foundation provide sufficient stability, a hoop may not be needed. Try embroidering without a hoop. If the stitches cause the fabrics to bunch, then use a hoop.

A favorite of mine that I find indispensable is a 14" round supported lap hoop, a quilter's hoop that is raised on supports above a base. This allows both hands to remain free for stitching. The heavy hoop accommodates all projects from silk to wool, and is especially beneficial for beading.

Laying Tool

Although not an essential tool, for fine silk thread and silk ribbon embroideries, a laying tool ensures that threads and ribbons will lie smoothly on the surface of the fabric. Have the project in a supported hoop so that both hands are free to stitch. Run the thread or ribbon over the laying tool while pulling the thread or ribbon to the back.

Iron and Ironing Board

Careful pressing while patching or piecing a crazy quilt helps to ensure a smooth quilt surface. Press patched quilt tops and embroideries face down on a towel if your ironing board is not padded.

Use a dry iron for hand patching to eliminate scorched fingers. For steam, use a spray bottle and spray the surface of the ironing board. To prevent water-spotting, do not spray the patch.

Use a press cloth on delicate fabrics and on those where pressing may cause a shiny surface.

I find a "wool" setting works well for most crazy patching purposes.

Sewing Machine

Unless you are going to do machine embroidery, a sewing machine with only a simple, straight stitch setting is necessary. If you patch a quilt by hand, all you need the machine for is to assemble the quilt in the end. It is nice to have a zigzag stitch in order to clean-finish edges, but even this is not necessary.

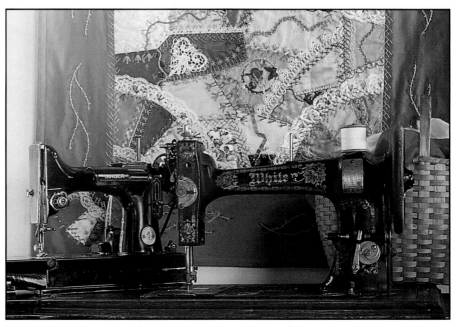

A treadle and an early Singer are still dependable workhorses today. A basket of silks awaits a new project.

A Workspace

For the patching part of crazy quilting, the placement of the ironing board is crucial to your set up. For hand patching a large quilt top, place the ironing board up to a table or desk so most of the foundation can be supported.

Lower the board to table height so you can work while comfortably seated.

For machine methods, place the board as near to the sewing machine as possible, even lowering it to desk-height so you can sew a seam and then press it while remaining seated.

Good lighting is very important. Choose fluorescent or incandescent lighting according to your preference. Color-corrected bulbs are nice, but not necessary. Use natural daylight to make color selections, then go ahead and work on your quilt under any kind of lighting.

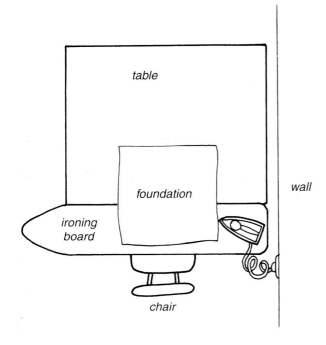

A table placed next to an ironing board is a convenient arrangement for patching a crazy quilt by hand.

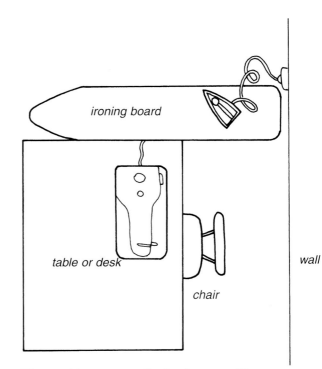

The machine-sewn methods of crazy quilting are easiest with an ironing board placed next to the sewing machine.

Crazy quilt detail. Photographed at Shiretown Antique Center, Alfred, Maine.

The "White Rose" quilt, 1862, with its many black-and-white patches is a strongly contrasting color scheme softened by touches of color. Photographed at Shiretown Antique Center, Alfred, Maine.

Natural Elegance

Victorian fabric types consisted of fibers that had been in use for ages: silk, cotton, linen and wool. Silks became especially popular since availability and affordability increased dramatically. And, the jacquard loom had been invented in the early 1800s, adding a new texture, woven-in patterning, to the mix.

In the late 1800s, in an attempt to imitate silk, it was discovered that rayons and acetate synthetics could be derived of natural materials. The original ones were highly flammable. But improved in the early 1900s, rayon fabrics are now invaluable for their beautiful finishes.

As William Henry Perkin was trying to make synthetic quinine, he accidentally discovered the color mauve, which in turn caused the invention of aniline dyes. With their creation, the Victorians had wider color ranges than with natural dyes, and at less expense.

Victorian ladies began to eschew the "old-fashioned" cotton calicoes, thinking them drab, and sought instead the new-fangled silks and other fancy types for their scrap quilts and crazy quilts.

Fabric Types for Crazy Quilting

The fabrics that work best for crazy patches, backings, and borders are the natural-fiber ones, plus rayon and acetate. It is useful to get to know the different fiber types and their characteristics.

Silk

The silk fiber has amazing strength, is translucent, and possesses a uniquely dry, crushy feel. It is a "protein" fiber, made of silkworm cocoons. These cocoons are unraveled into a fine strand called "filament" silk, which is then plied into threads. In comparison, "spun" silks are carded and spun. The filament silks are capable of the highest sheen, while spun silks tend to be matte or nearly matte in finish.

Habotai, taffeta, jacquard, charmeuse, satin, dupioni, noil, and velvet are some of the many weaves and fabric types in which silk is available. Silk fabrics can be crisp as taffeta, or soft and nearly weightless as Habotai. Finishes vary from matte to shiny and smooth to coarse, depending on the preparation of the silk and the weave of the fabric.

Silk in its natural state is washable, although when washed for the first time, shrinkage can occur and some dyes, especially darker colors, may run. Silk garments and yardage labeled "dry-clean only" may not be colorfast and could shrink. Some surface finishes can change with washing. As with other fabric types, test-wash a small piece before immersing the whole piece.

Wash silk in lukewarm water with mild soap, and line dry. Press on low heat to prevent scorching. If the fabric is crumpled up and wrinkles have set in, apply steam or mist while ironing. Should static occur, try misting the air with water.

Cotton

Cotton comes from the seed head that forms on the plant after the flower blooms. In its natural state, it is a matte fiber. However, mercerization, invented in the mid-1800s, is a process that treats cotton with caustic soda, producing high luster, greater strength, and more efficient dye absorption.

Some of the finishes and weaves associated with cottons include broadcloth, twill, velveteen, gauze, and corduroy. Cotton moiré and chintz have polished surfaces produced by running the fabric through rollers, although these glossy surfaces have a tendency to wash out. Cotton fabric types vary from lightweight to heavy and from sheer to opaque. Since the fiber itself is opaque, sheerness is obtained by using fine threads and/or open weaves.

Cotton fabrics can be washed with agitation in hot or cold water.

"Satin" is a weave, not a fiber type. The satin weave creates floats of threads on the surface of the fabric that reflect the light. Satins are made out of silk, cotton, acetate, or polyester fibers. Silk satin is the most luxurious of them all, with its lustrous surface and beautiful drape. Cotton satin (sateen) has a beautiful finish that is ideal for crazy patches and finishing quilts. Cotton sateen was a utilitarian fabric in Victorian times, frequently used for borders, backings, and patches in antique crazy quilts.

Some shrinkage in the first washing is normal, as is the loss of excess dye. Press cottons on high heat using steam.

Linen

Linen comes from the flax plant. Preparing the plant for fabric production is a laborious process that involves rotting away the non-fibrous parts of the plant, and then the resulting fibers are spun and woven. Linen can be woven into fine handkerchief linens, or coarser fabrics and canvas.

Linens often have a distinctive luster, especially when starched and pressed. Because it is a firm fiber, it makes an ideal evenweave fabric for cross-stitch embroidery … and adds beautiful texture in crazy patchwork.

A long-lasting fiber (Egyptian mummies were wrapped in it), linen tends to have a feel of age-old elegance. Linen is washable and can be pressed on high heat.

Rayon

First appearing in the late 1800s, rayon is the result of a search for synthetic silk. Rayon consists of cellulose fibers derived from wood or cottonseed, making it uniquely both synthetic and natural.

One of its best qualities is that it is capable of a high sheen, although matte finishes are also available. Another fine quality is its drape (see the Piano Shawl, page 135). Rayon is used in combination with silk to make velvet. Another fabric—bengaline—consists of rayon woven over a cotton core.

Rayon presses easily and holds a crease even with finger-pressing. For this reason, the closely-woven types are excellent for appliqué. Use cool temps for washing, and press on low heat. Handle with care because rayon weakens when wet, but it firms up again once it is dried.

Acetate

Acetate, also synthesized of cellulose, is an offshoot of the rayon discovery. Not used commercially until 1924, it is often woven into satin or taffeta fabrics. Taffeta is sometimes run through rollers to give it a moiré finish. The satin has a high luster and a firm drape. This fabric is crisp and, when rubbed against itself, tends to be noisy.

Often sold as "dry clean only," these fabrics are handwashable although washing may cut the shine on some finishes. If you do handwash them, do not wring them; acetates easily crease. Line dry, and press on low heat.

Wool

A century ago, there may have been many crazy quilts made of wool. Those I have found are mostly bed-size and well worn.

Wool fabrics vary from finely-woven challis to heavy types for coats and blankets. Suit-weights and challis make excellent crazy patches. Most patterned wool fabrics are woven-in plaids, herringbones, and pinstripes. Natural sheep-color browns, grays, tans, and off-whites are lovely and useful neutral shades.

Wool holds a crease when steamed and allows sculptural forming by steaming (hats are an example). Wash wool by soaking it (see washing instructions below), because agitation will cause it to felt. Keep the water the same temperature when washing and rinsing, as *changes* in temperature cause shrinkage.

Washing Instructions

If you are not sure about the washability of a fabric, first test-wash a small piece. This allows you to observe if the fabric dulls, bleeds dye, or shrinks excessively.

1. *Use cool to lukewarm water and mild soap.*
2. *Cottons can be washed vigorously, but all other fabric types should be soaked instead.*
3. *Rinse by repeatedly changing the water until it is clear. Use the same temperature as for washing. If dyes are running, keep rinsing to see if they stop. If not, the fabric is not colorfast and should not be washed.*
4. *Do not wring. Instead, wrap the fabrics in a large towel, roll, and gently squeeze. Line dry.*
5. *Press at an appropriate temperature and, if necessary, use steam.*

Mary's Velvet Dilemma

Mary sent this tale of woe spontaneously out to nearly 700 members of the Quiltropolis.com e-mail list:

"I was rummaging around today at a yard sale and got a *wonderful* beautiful deep blue velvet coat with a furry white lining and ivory satin sleeves. What a find! Ran home, jumped on the bed with a cup of coffee, the TV clicky dude, and scissors! Took me the better part of two hours but finally I had everything whacked up.

"Of course at this point, I have my tissues because there's little tiny, tiny, nanno-tiny white hairs everywhere … I'm sneezing … the Pupper is sneezing … I run downstairs, throw the blue velvet in the washer.

"Took out a huge knot of string and velvet— gggGGRRRrrr—stand there and untangle.

"Throw in (the dryer) to soften and unwrinkle. Pupper now wants out and the phone rings … grab tissues … finally make it back to the dryer, open the door and fluff out bitty blue fluffles everywhere … The inside of the door is solid with blue … I'm sneezing, the Pupper is sneezing … I've sworn the Pupper to silence or no doggie treats! Lesson learned: Don't cut up velvet *before* washing!"

reprinted by permission of Mary Weinberg.

Fabrics from worn kimonos can provide inspiration for a quilt. Adapt the designs on dishes and pottery for embroidery motifs.

Shopping for Fabrics

Crazy quilting is an excellent opportunity to explore fabrics and colors, and shopping and collecting can be as inspiring as diving into a new project. The right piece of fabric often can inspire an entire project. Search fabric stores for clothing and bridal types, quilt shops for cotton solids. Interesting fabrics can be found in upholstery and drapery shops, but collect only those that are lightweight enough to be hemmed easily. Seek out shops that sell remnants and mill ends, where interesting fabrics can often be found, although they may be unlabeled. If you know the different fiber types, it is often possible to determine what they are. (Hint: synthetics tend to melt under a hot iron.)

Look for all-cotton sheets for borders and backings. Check out linen selections for damask and lace tablecloths. Look in second-hand shops and yard sales for rarely-worn evening and tailored wear. Search for men's ties, especially silk ones.

Also consider buying white or natural-color silk yardage and dyeing it as an easy way to achieve a wide range of colors.

Choose wovens (not knits which can stretch and bag). Choose textured fabrics rather than prints for embroidery to show up well.

Tips for Collecting

- Buy what you like when you see it. If you go back for it later, it may not be there.
- Save scraps down to the smallest possible patch-size pieces, especially luxury fabrics such as silks. Use them in miniature quilts, and for making covered buttons and fabric flowers.
- Buy new to have the old: Buy the man in your life a new tie and then talk him out of an old one.
- Recycle still-good, older clothing into patches.
- Ask for donations from friends and family.

There is a balance between warm and cool shades (red and blue) in this antique wool quilt. Detail. The Brick Store Museum, Kennebunk, Maine.

Choosing Colors

Selecting a combination of coordinating colors can be one of the most baffling aspects of a crazy quilting project. A basic understanding of color theory can be helpful.

The colors used in beautiful antique crazy quilts are worth considering. Observe the photos of antique quilts throughout this book and you will see that there is a lot of contrast in these quilts: The colors range from very light to very dark.

Also, darks, lights, and neutral shades are often used nearly equally. This creates an overall balance, making the quilt easy to look at even if the maker used many colors. In addition, there tends to be nearly equal amounts of warm and cool shades.

Bright golden yellow was used in some Victorian crazy quilts in occasional patches. It is also found in embroidery, and was sometimes used as the sole embroidery thread color. This yellow, used with other jewel-like and deep tones such as burgundy, dark green, violet, red, and blue, adds a wonderful touch of contrast and brightness.

This circa mid-19th century quilt is made of many mauve, magenta, and purple fabrics. Some of the patches are set into a "sidewalk" pattern! Detail. The Brick Store Museum, Kennebunk, Maine.

Color Pointers Taken from Antique Quilts

- Use vivid colors sparingly (magenta, royal blue, yellow, etc.), separating them with plenty of neutrals or with darker or lighter colors.

- To avoid a monotonous and dull appearance, separate similar shades (such as faded shades of rose and blue) with lights or darks.

- Use a black patch to highlight nearby colors. Black patches in antique quilts were often embroidered with florals or painted.

- Use shades of brown to harmonize surrounding colors. Browns tend to assume the depth of warm colors and the coolness of cool ones. Browns will tend to "extend" a color scheme, rather than change it.

Color Theory
Primary and Secondary Colors

The primary colors are red, blue, and yellow, and they are the basis for all other colors. The secondary colors are obtained by mixing two primary colors, as shown in the diagram.

Tertiary Colors

As is evident in their names, the tertiary colors are obtained by mixing a secondary color with a primary: Yellow/green, for instance, is made of yellow and green.

There are variations on each. For example, a yellow/green that tends toward yellow is yellow/yellow/green.

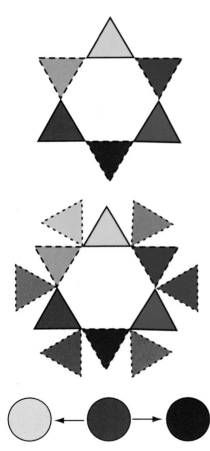

Adding white or black to a color creates an infinite range of possibilities. When using dyes, the addition of water substitutes for the color white.

Choosing a certain grouping of colors from a color wheel creates color schemes.

Using various shades of one color is a monochromatic color scheme. This is the simplest color scheme possible. Add one or more neutrals.

Analogous colors share characteristics. Red, red/orange, and orange are united by the varying degrees of red in each of these colors. Blue-green (peacock), green-blue (teal), and green are united by the common element of green. The analogous colors naturally blend. They easily complete a color scheme when lighter, darker, and neutral shades are added.

Complementary colors are a combination of two colors that have no shared characteristics. Red and green are commonly used complementaries. The color green is obtained by mixing yellow and blue, neither of which appears in red—a primary or pure hue. Purple and yellow are complimentary (purple consists of red and blue, and yellow is a pure hue), as are blue and orange (orange is yellow plus red and blue is a pure hue).

Complementary colors are easily found on a color wheel as direct opposites. There are also in-between complementary hues, such as blue-violet and yellow-orange. When placed next to each other, vivid complementary colors tend to "clash" or reverberate. Use them to create vibrant areas in a quilt. In one antique crazy quilt, I saw a large fan pieced of royal blue and orange, a striking combination!

When the colors are muted, complementaries blend nicely.

Cool colors include blues, purples, and blue-greens. Cool colors tend to portray restful, calm, peaceful, and relaxed feelings.

Warm colors, indicative of action and passion, include reds, yellows, oranges, and yellow-greens.

Neutral colors include shades of brown, gray, gray-browns (taupes), black and white. The browns are various mixtures of the pure hues mentioned above. Grays are mixtures of white and black.

When used between other colors in a quilt, browns and grays tend to create restful areas. Both prevent strong colors from overpowering.

A balanced color scheme is the hallmark of this elegant, mid- to late-19th century crazy quilt. Many neutrals soften bright colors. Detail. The Brick Store Museum, Kennebunk, Maine.

Choosing Colors in Nature

We live in a colorful world! We are accustomed to an array of colors. How much do we actually think about them?

Many of us may have learned color "prejudices" at an early age. For instance, while in Kindergarten we were taught that tree trunks are brown. In reality, tree trunks are shades of gray, taupe, and olive. Most unlike the blue crayon so singularly used, the colors of lake, ocean, and sky are ever-changing.

Notice how nature imposes vast areas in shades such as greens and blues. How much sky is there in comparison to everything else? How do these panoramas function as backdrops for the colorful accents of flowers and birds?

Looking into the distance, what happens to the colors of objects? Do they fade, pale, or take on grayed shades?

Compare the effects on a particular scene on a gray day and a sunny day, or perhaps a scene through a window. What colors are the shadows? Is there inspiration here to translate to a quilt, an embroidery for a patch, or a color scheme?

My favorite place to observe colors is the flower garden. Each day there is something new to behold. From vivid spring crocus to heady lilac panicles, followed by soft sprays of baby's breath blooming one day and fading the next, the garden is a summer-long orchestra of colors. When roses bloom, each petal is a wonder to observe. What a surprise when the yellow and black spider has spun its fabulous web overnight. Drops of dew glitter on the web—what a sight to see, and to embroider, perhaps?

Compare the effect of a glossy-leafed plant to one with a soft, fuzzy leaf. Bring these textures to a quilt you are working on! How can you replicate them with your fabric choices? Observe also the wildlife attracted to the garden. Birds, insects, butterflies, and toads: Each of these is a study in colors and textures.

Interior decorating and clothing fads and fashions over the years have combined colors in different ways. These are also opportunities to observe and study colors. Everywhere you go, see how colors were used in the exteriors and interiors of buildings. Go to museums to observe how colors were once used in clothing and upholstery. Studying colors and textures will heighten your awareness and appreciation of them.

Garden spiders appear in late summer to spin their elegant webs.

Exercise: Have you ever said: "I *hate* that color," or is there a color that is not "your" color and you won't use it for anything? What color is it—chartreuse, fuchsia, an off-shade of green, perhaps? Find a piece of fabric in that color. Choose surrounding patch colors that look pretty to you, using neutrals if no others will do. Add a bit of lace to soften, do a little embroidery on it—a small butterfly, perhaps, or some silk ribbon roses.

Do you find yourself beginning to like a color you once thought you didn't like or couldn't use? Continue this exercise with any other disliked colors. Believe it or not, your color horizons will expand. You will start to look at colors with an eye to "where and how can I use that shade?" instead of saying "yuck."

antique crazy quilt was made in long strips with velvet sashings. The sole embroidery is a chenille that appears to consist of metallic
s couched along the patch edges. Photographed at Gold Bug Antiques, Cape Neddick, Maine.

Foundation Piecing

Victorian crazy quilts were intentionally made, they were not "over-patched," worn-out quilts, nor were they leftover sewing scraps simply plunked down and embroidered in place. Patterns for crazy patched blocks, as well as scrap bag packages of fabrics, were sold specifically for crazy quilting.

In Victorian times, there were many influences that could have inspired crazy quilting. In England, the Great Exhibition of 1851, housed in the temporary Crystal Palace, brought together examples of the arts and industries of many nations. Trade with the Orient flourished and influenced Western art and decorating trends. Some believe that crazy patching may have been inspired by the crackled, aged glazes on antique pottery, or cracked glass or ice. There are many other possibilities that may have inspired the "crazed" look including paving stones, stone walls, and patterns in nature. Somehow, quilters were influenced to get "out of the box" of geometric piecing and so, for a while, explored the alternatives.

The reverse side of a block from a crazy quilt that was never assembled clearly shows that foundation patching was intentional. The backs of the embroidery stitches and some basting indicate the Antique Method of crazy quilting. This block is 9" square. Collection of the author.

The right side of the block.

Foundation Fabrics

Except for the Confetti Piecing Method, crazy quilting consists of applying patches of varying sizes and shapes onto a foundation, a piece of fabric the size of the quilt top or block. A foundation fabric should be chosen for the desired qualities that it would add to the finished quilt or project, such as drape, warmth, weight, and/or firmness.

Muslin

An excellent choice for beginners, 100 percent cotton muslin provides a firm base, and can be used with any patching method. It is excellent for quilt tops and many projects, but is not always the best choice for garments, since it provides little drape. Look for a quality pre-shrunk, unbleached muslin with an even grain.

Batiste

A soft, finely-woven, lightweight fabric, 100 percent cotton batiste is perfect for shawls, drapey quilts, and clothing. To retain the drape, pair it with soft and lightweight silks and cottons, and challis-type patch fabrics. Because of its softness, it is liable to bunch. Careful patching and pressing, and using an embroidery hoop for all embroidery and embellishment can prevent this.

Silk Organza

Crisp, loosely-woven, and nearly weightless, silk organza is an ideal foundation for all-silk quilts, garments, or lightweight projects. The fabric shrinks significantly in pre-washing, so be sure to buy extra yardage. Square up the organza along a table edge or cutting mat to keep its grain even while patching. After basting, it will hold its shape. Use an embroidery hoop for embroidery and sewn embellishment.

Flannel

Cotton flannel doubles as both a lightweight batting and foundation. It is excellent used in wool quilts and jackets for extra warmth. As with batiste, check often for bunching because this fabric is soft.

This aged cotton crazy quilt consists of blocks separated by sashings. Detail courtesy of The Kirk Collection, Omaha, Nebraska. Photo by Nancy T. Kirk.

Preparing the Foundation

Always pre-wash the foundation fabric. Wash cottons in hot, soapy water. Wash silk organza by hand in warm water with mild soap. Rinse well, line-dry, and press. Cut the foundation to the size of the quilt top or block including any seam allowances. Trim off any selvedges that prevent the fabric from lying flat.

Whole Quilt Crazy Quilts

The whole quilt style is useful for smaller quilts such as crib, lap robes, throws, and wall quilts. For larger pieces, patching and embroidery may be cumbersome (although not impossible). I often use a square or rectangle based on the width of the foundation fabric. For instance, 44" wide foundation makes a 44" square or rectangular quilt top (including seam allowances).

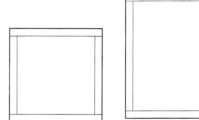

In this 1928 block-style wool quilt, the blocks are staggered. Collection of Rocky Mountain Quilts, York Village, Maine.

A foundation can be of any shape. This "butterfly" is thought to be an unassembled purse. Photographed at The Barn at Cape Neddick, Maine.

The Block Style of Crazy Quilting

Dividing the quilt top into blocks creates manageable portions. Make blocks from about 12" to 18-22" square, depending upon your preferences.

The blocks do not have to be square or all the same size as long as they fit together in the end. A large, central block can be surrounded by smaller blocks. You can also make them into hexagons or diamonds.

If you want the whole quilt effect, allow some patches to hang over the edges and then appliqué them later onto the adjoining blocks.

After the blocks are patched and embroidered, machine sew them with right sides together, then press the seams open. These seams can be embroidered with feather or other stitching, taking care to keep the seam allowances open and flat.

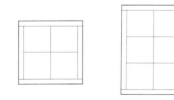

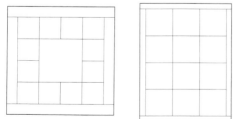

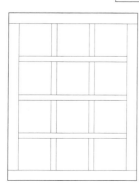

Crazy patches were machine stitched into diamond-shaped blocks in this vintage crazy quilt. Collection of Rocky Mountain Quilts, York Village, Maine.

Blocks can also be assembled with sashing between them, as in the Cousins quilt (see page 139).

Cutting Patches

Patches are not cut ahead of time. Cut each as it is needed according to the instructions for the method you are using.

What sizes to make the patches depends on personal preference, the project, and available fabric. If you are a beginner, larger patches will be easier and reduce patching time. If embroidery or embellishment will be worked on the centers of patches, be sure they are large enough for this.

Bunching

"Bunching" refers to patches and foundations that do not lie

smoothly. Either the patch was not laid evenly, or the foundation shifted, causing fabrics to ripple, bulge, or pucker. Napped fabrics, such as velveteens, are sometimes the culprits. To prevent bunching, be sure the foundation remains smooth (lift your work and check it), pin carefully, hand baste, and press often.

Bunching can also happen when using a sewing machine. This shrinks the size of the finished piece, making it uneven, and causing a poor fit when blocks are assembled. To prevent this, hold the fabric firmly both in front of and behind the needle while sewing.

You can cut the foundation larger to accommodate any shrinkage, but with careful work the problem can be avoided.

Beautiful, heirloom-quality trims add touches of elegance to a crazy quilt. Cotton net lace, cotton and rayon Venice laces, cotton eyelet, and several narrow trims are shown here.

Basting

Basting is done after a block, or whole quilt top or a section of it is patched and pinned.

Lightly press the pinned patches, making sure that everything lies smoothly. Double check that patches are sufficiently overlapped with no foundation showing through any gaps.

Basting should be done on a flat surface (preferably a cutting mat) to prevent scratching your table. Start in one area and work outward. Baste each turned-under edge.

Use a size 12 Sharp, or other hand sewing needle. Thread the needle with basting thread or cotton sewing thread. Knot the end.

Take several stitches then pull the thread through. In stitching, the needle slides along the working surface. Keep the piece flat. As you work, continually check that patches stay smooth. Stitches can be of any size that results in a smoothly secured patch. Mine are about ½" in length.

If the piece tends to slide around as you work on it, weight it with books or objects that won't harm the fabrics.

Patched and ready for embroidery and embellishment, the Ladies and Fans quilt is clothes-pinned to hangers for viewing.

Viewing Your Work

After basting all of the patches in place, I like to hang the piece to be able to view it from a distance. An easy way to do this is to clip it to coat hangers using smooth, spring-type clothespins. Use as many hangers as needed, and bend the tops so they fit over a door or curtain rod. This is a great way to store the piece when you are not working on it.

Patching Methods

Each of the following four methods comes out a little differently. A Potholder pattern follows, a small project with which you can try each of the methods.

The Antique Method

This is how most of the antique crazy quilts were made. Curved-edge patches are easy to do, creating a softer effect than with all angular patches. Begin from a corner, or anywhere you like. Patching can be started in several different areas at once, which come together as patches are added. For some patching ideas, refer to Embroidery Stitches on pages 34 to 73.

1. Cut and lay a patch wherever you'd like to begin—at a corner, an edge, or in the center of the foundation.

2. Lay a second patch under- or overlapping it with the first by ½"

or a little more. Repeat with the third and fourth patches. Continue to add patches in the same way. Pin each as it is laid. If the patching area is large, you may wish to patch only an area of the foundation, then press and baste the patches (see steps 3 and 4), before continuing on.

3. Go back to the first patch laid, and press under its overlapped edges about ¼" and pin. Continue to press and pin each patch. Afterwards, if any gaps have appeared where the foundation shows through, fit in an extra patch, replace a patch with a larger one, or add a piece of wide ribbon.

4. Pin on any desired laces or trims, securing them into seam allowances. Baste all patch edges (see page 21), then embroider and embellish.

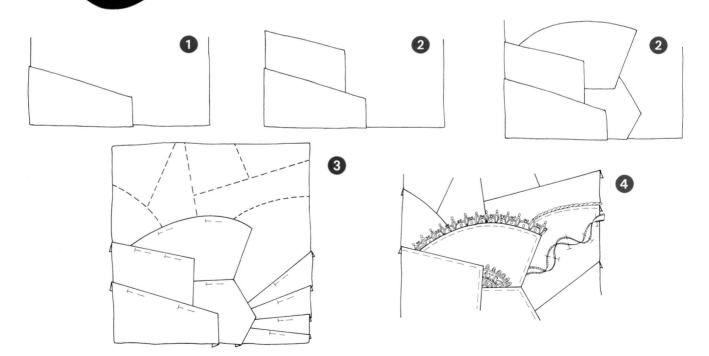

If patching gets puzzling and you become confused as to what to do next, here are some suggestions that may help:
Take a break and come back later with a fresh mind.
If you were painstakingly trying to fit small pieces together, set them aside and use one larger piece instead. Or sew several small ones together and then add them as one.
Begin anew on a different area of the foundation, and work toward the original area.

Landscape Patching Method

A variation of the Antique Method, the Landscape Patching Method is a little easier because there is no need to figure out which edges will be turned under. Each patch is "finished" as it is added. Patches tend to "landscape," creating the effect of rolling hills or mountain ranges. Varying the sizes of patches, and making some long and narrow, and some more square-shaped can downplay this effect.

Lay patches as if you were painting with fabric instead of paint. Arrange and rearrange until the composition feels "right," then pin the fabrics in place. Trims are being added to this landscape piece.

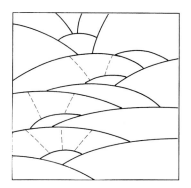

This landscaped block was designed to achieve the effect of rolling hills. The dashed lines indicate patches that were pieced together before being added. Turn the page sideways, and then upside down to see the different effects that can be achieved by the orientation of the block.

1. Beginning at one corner, cut a patch with a rounded edge, or a square with one corner removed. Press under all edges except those that will become the sides of the block. Pin it to the foundation.

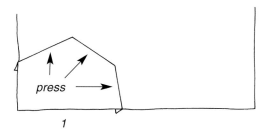

2. Cut the next patch so that one edge can be tucked, and the others pressed under. Press under all but the tucked edge, and insert it under the first patch. Pin. Continue in this manner, trimming out any excess seam allowances (leaving at least ¼").

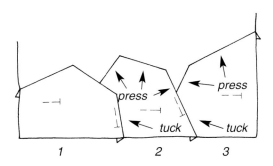

3. Pin on any desired trimmings. Baste all patch edges (see page 21) then embroider and embellish.

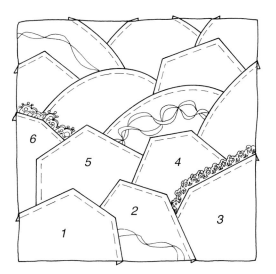

Sew-N-Flip Machine Patching Method

Have your ironing board placed next to your sewing machine. You will want to work with blocks that are not too large or the piece will become difficult to handle. A good size to begin with is about 10" to 12" square. Use a firm foundation such as muslin. It is easiest to work with patches that have straight sides, and cut into triangular or long, sloping rectangular shapes. Curved shapes can be added—the curved edges must be pressed under and sewn by hand. If you are adding laces and trims, remember to sew them into the seams of the patches as you go.

1. Begin with a five-sided patch at the center of the block. Pin. Lay a second patch onto the first with right sides together, and sew the seam, leaving ¼" unsewn at each end. Do not backstitch, since occasionally part of a seam may need to be opened up later on.

2. Add each patch in this manner, trimming out any excess from previous patches. Where edges cannot be sewn by machine, including curved edges, turn them under and press. These edges can later be slipstitched, or held in place with embroidery.

3. As patches are added, the new ones are generally made longer to fit onto several earlier ones. To prevent a "convoluted Log Cabin" look, piece two or three fabrics

together, then sew on as one (see patches 6, 8, and 10 in the diagram).

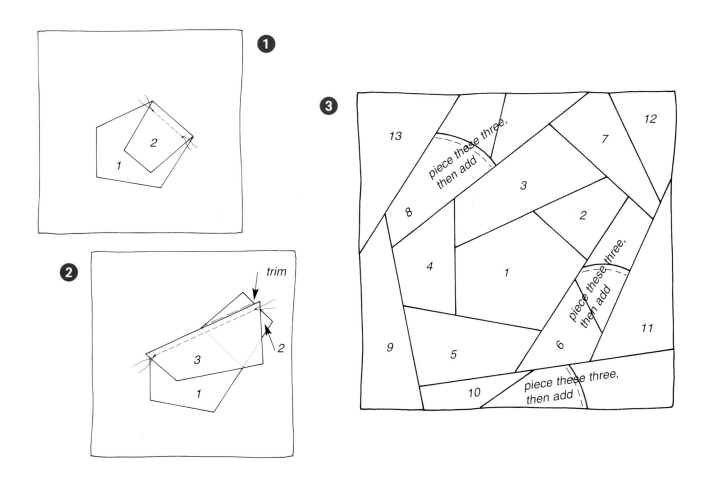

Confetti Piecing Method

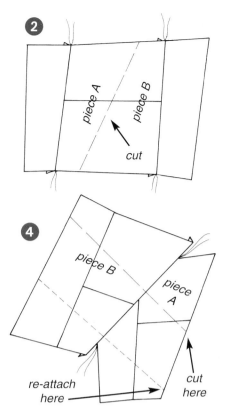

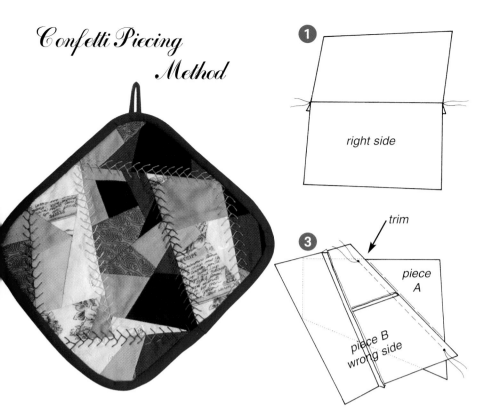

Confetti piecing is quicker and easier than Sew-N-Flip. It is done completely by machine, without a foundation, and results in all straight seams. Cotton fabrics are recommended. Although it can be accomplished by using a scissors and ruler, it is easiest to use a rotary cutter, acrylic ruler, and a cutting mat. In order to understand how the method works, first do a "test-run" with scrap fabrics. Use ¼" seam allowances, pressing to one side.

1. Sew together two large patches that are 9" x 11" or so. Press. Add a patch to each end as shown. Sew and press.

2. Cut the piece in half along a straight line.

3. Turn the two pieces, and rejoin by sewing, having right sides together. Press.

4. Cut again, and rejoin. When rejoining two pieces, it is not necessary to rejoin at an edge. With right sides together, add the second piece anywhere onto the first and then trim off the excess. Rejoin the trimmed-off piece to another area.

To use eight colors, make two pieces as in step 1, using eight different fabrics. In the process of cutting and sewing, join the two blocks until the colors are effectively distributed.

As you cut and sew, begin to form the piece into a square or rectangle that is larger than the size of the block you wish to have. When finished, cut out the block, making sure to add seam allowances.

Embroidery along seams is optional. If you wish to embroider along the patch seams, first baste a muslin foundation onto the back.

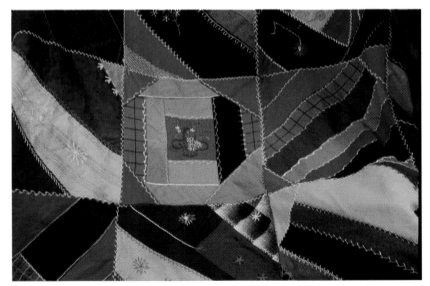

These 11½" square blocks were patched in a simple manner. Detail. Owned by Avalon Antiques, photographed at Arundel Antiques in Arundel, Maine. Photo by Paul Baresel.

Making a Pattern

If it is easier for you to follow patterns instead of free-handing the patching process, here is how to make them.

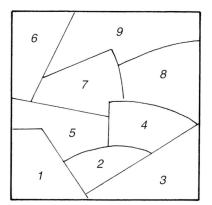

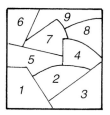

1. You will need a piece of paper the size of the finished block (without seam allowances).

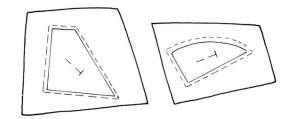

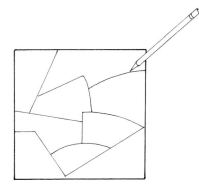

2. For patch ideas, refer to the Embroidery Stitches section on pages 34 to 73. Sketch the patch outlines onto the paper. Use a ruler for straight lines, and freehand the curves. Erase and re-work the design until you have a balanced arrangement.

3. Cut a piece of muslin for the foundation ¼" larger all around than the size of the block.
Cut out one of the paper patches and pin it onto a piece of scrap fabric. Cut out the patch, adding seam allowances all around of at least ¼". Lay the patch onto the muslin foundation.

Continue to cut paper and fabric patches, adding them to the muslin. Sew them on if using the Sew-N-Flip Method, otherwise proceed as for the Antique Method.

Potholder Pattern

Try each of the four patching methods by making a set of potholders. Finished size of each: 8½" square. Use a ¼" seam allowance throughout.

Instructions

1. If desired, round the corners of muslin, batting, and backing pieces. Apply patches to each of three muslin pieces, using the Antique Method for one, Landscape for another, and Sew-N-Flip Method for the third. Construct a fourth using the Confetti Piecing Method, and baste the muslin on afterwards.

2. Embroider along patch seams as desired.

3. Assemble the layers: quilted top, batting, backing. Pin.

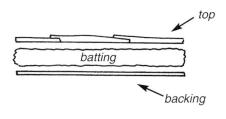

4. Sew a loop for each potholder out of the bias tape, and baste to one corner of each.

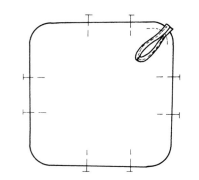

5. Open out the bias tape and sew it with right sides together ¼" from the edge of the potholder. Ease the bias at the corners so it will turn smoothly. When you've sewn all the way around, overlap onto the beginning and then fold the end under. Fold the bias to the back, press, and slipstitch.

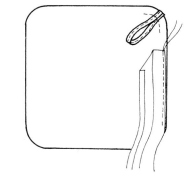
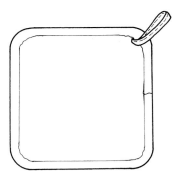

Materials

Four 9" squares of muslin

8 or more patch fabrics

Cotton laces as desired

Four 9" squares of 100 percent cotton batting

Four 9" squares of cotton or linen backing fabric

Size 8 pearl cotton, 8 or more colors

5 yards of ½" wide double-folded bias tape

Sewing thread

Crazy quilt detail. Collection of Rocky Mountain Quilts, York Village, Maine.

There is a range of embroidery stitches in this circa 1880s crazy quilt. The Brick Store Museum, Kennebunk, Maine.

Chapter 2

Victorian Stitches

Both practical and aesthetic, the rows of embroidery stitches along the patch seams of antique crazy quilts fasten the patches to each other and at the same time quilt them to the foundation fabric. Although many Victorian crazy quilts featured a single row of feather or herringbone stitches, fancier ones have a wide variety of stitches, and sometimes multiple rows along each seam. The almost facet-like patterning of some of these quilts makes them seem to sparkle.

According to Betsey Telford of Rocky Mountain Quilts in York, Maine, the mark of excellence in Victorian crazy quilting was to make at least one hundred different stitches on a quilt.

Twisted threads impart an unrivaled texture and definition to stitches worked along patch seams. Vikki Clayton's hand-dyed Spun Silk Perle, size 8 pearl cotton, Kreinik's Silk Serica, YLI Pearl Crown Rayon, and buttonhole silks are some of the twisted threads that work well for patch seam embroidery.

Threads for Crazy Quilting

Collect a variety of the many wonderful thread types available, and try them. You're sure to find some that will become your favorites.

Silk, cotton, wool, rayon, blended fiber, and synthetic threads are available in a variety of sizes and finishes. Silk, rayon, and metallic threads are spun of many short fibers, or made of long singular filaments. Cotton and wool threads are always spun, since their

fibers by nature are short. Spun fibers are often more matte in finish, while filaments display more sheen.

Twisted Threads for Patch Seam Embroidery

Twisted threads have a distinctive texture and quality that makes them perfect for embroidery along patch seams. They are not flosses, and are not separated into

strands. There are many beautiful ones available, providing a range of sizes. You can mix and match different threads on one quilt, or choose one to use exclusively.

The most common and the easiest threads for beginners are the pearl (or perle) cottons. Size 8 is a commonly used size, and is available in a wide range of colors. Size 5 is heavier if you prefer a thicker thread. Use size 12 or flower thread for finer uses, such as miniature quilts.

Some of the twisted silks include Soie Perlee and buttonhole silk, both of which are of "average"

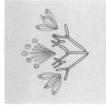

What is a ply, and what is a strand? These two terms are often confused with each other. A ply is a single strand spun of filament fiber or thread. For instance, sewing thread is one strand, however if you untwist the end of it you will see that the thread divides into separate plies. Plies are not meant to be separated. A strand is one thread of several that are placed together to form a multi-strand skein such as six-strand embroidery floss. A combination of twist and plies are what give a thread its strength.

Threads for working embroideries include The Caron Collection's Waterlilies and Impressions, spooled silks for machine embroideries, Kreinik's Silk Mori, Soie Perlee, flower thread, and wool threads.

Variety threads, braids, and ribbons add dimension and texture. Some can be sewn through fabric; others can be couched onto the surface. Shown here are Kreinik metallic braids, cords, and ribbons; YLI silk ribbons; mohair yarn; Japan gold and silver; chenilles and other exotic types.

Threads for Other Uses

For working embroideries in patch centers, flosses are ideal. They can be found in cotton, silk, rayon, and metallic fibers. Cotton flosses are commonly found in many stores. Soie D'Alger and Silk Mori are two examples of silk flosses, available in wide color ranges. An excellent hand-dyed floss is Waterlilies. There are many more silk flosses available in twisted, lightly twisted, and untwisted forms for matte to shiny finishes.

Wool threads are ideal for both patch seam and patch embroideries on wool and other quilts. Persian wool has separable strands, and Broder Medici is a single-strand finer wool. For a touch of luxury, try Impressions, a 50 percent silk /50 percent wool thread available in many hand-dyed colors.

This Oriental silk embroidery is a gorgeous example of satin stitch embroidery.

thickness. The heavier thread, Silk Serica, is a little more distinctive if you prefer a thread that stands out well. Lighter-weight silks include Silk Bella and Soie Gobelin. There are other threads, including a line called "Tire" available in a range of thickness on spools that are handy for machine work. Vikki Clayton's hand-dyed silk perles in luscious colors are offered in several weights, and in filament or spun (softer) types.

An outstanding rayon thread is Pearl Crown Rayon, wonderful for its sheen, and similar in weight to size 8 pearl cotton. There is a good range of colors, and the spools are large so they last.

Metallic threads often consist of a tinsel-like strand that is spun, plied, or wound around a core of nylon or other fiber. There are many types from one-ply filaments to twisted threads and flosses, cording, and ribbons that can be couched. Blending filaments are very fine and are meant to be knotted into the needle alongside a second thread of a different type.

Yarns such as angora, alpaca, and mohair can be used creatively in embroideries or for couching along patch seams.

Chenille is a yarn with a pile spun into its core threads. Chenilles were popular Victorian embroidery materials, couched as filler in embroideries, or along patch seams.

Tips for Working with Threads

- A working length of thread is up to a yard for most cottons, and about 18" for threads that are problematic.

- If a thread frays at the needle's eye, pull it a little through the needle and trim off the frayed end. If it keeps happening, discard the needle—it may be defective.

- Twisted silk thread can snag, pulling one ply loose, and causing the thread to appear to disintegrate right before your eyes. If this should happen, hold the thread vertically and drop the needle to where it comes through the fabric. Run your fingers upward along the thread several times, smoothing it until the plies become even. Bring the needle back up and continue stitching.

- To prepare flosses for embroidery when more than one strand will be used, they should first be stripped. Cut a working length and then individually pull out as many strands as needed. Lay them back together smoothly. This allows the fullest sheen of the thread to show.

- Rayon threads often benefit from being given a quick snap before using. This relaxes the fibers, helping to prevent tangling.

- To remove the kinkiness from skeined rayon threads, run the thread over a damp towel and allow it to dry before using.

- Tangling is a common problem with any embroidery threads. Hold up your work and allow the thread to dangle and untwist occasionally.

- If threads "wear" as you use them, do not "sew" with them. Make the stitch in parts, pulling the thread all the way through each time. Also use short lengths of thread.

- If your fingers keep snagging the threads, apply a non-greasy hand lotion, then buff your hands on a clean towel until they feel smooth and dry. Keep an emery board handy to smooth any recurring rough spots.

- Begin and end threads in ways other than using knots. Take several tiny stitches on the back, or work threads into the backs of previously made stitches.

If you learn only one stitch, such as the plain feather stitch, that is all you need to complete a quilt top. After you become proficient with one stitch, try learning another. Antique block, 9" square. Collection of the author.

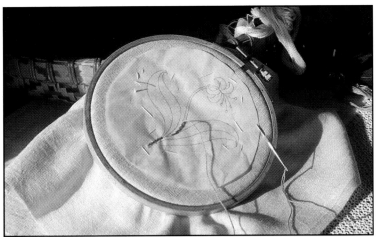

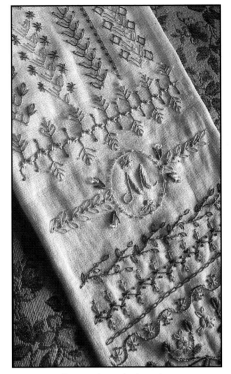

The Tracing Paper Transfer Method is easy, effective, and leaves no marks on the fabric.

The Tracing Paper Transfer Method

I thought I had invented this method, but then found it in Erica Wilson's books on embroidery! It has been a foolproof way to get designs onto crazy patches without leaving permanent marks on the fabric. It is ideal for almost any embroidery design.

Using a hard lead pencil, trace the design onto artist's tracing paper. The hard lead is important, because soft leads can coat the threads as you stitch.

Cut out the tracing, leaving an extra ½" of tissue all around. Place the fabric or quilt top into an embroidery hoop. The best hoop for this is a quilter's lap hoop, because it provides a large working area and keeps the fabric stable as you work. Baste the tracing onto the fabric.

Embroider the outlines of the design and then carefully tear away the tracing paper. With very intricate designs, you may need to use a tweezers to remove all bits of paper. Finish the embroidery.

Tissue wrapping paper can also be used. It is less durable and pencil lines may not show up as well, but is easier to remove afterwards.

Learning the Embroidery Stitches

Most stitches are easy to learn, although some may appear more complicated than they actually are. Begin with the simpler ones, working your way gradually into the more intricate-looking ones. "Variations and Combinations" are given to show some of many ways to use the stitches along patch edges. Experiment with using two or three stitches per row, with each in a different color.

A way to learn the stitches is to create a sampler on evenweave linen fabric. Make the stitches evenly by following the weave of the fabric.

Catherine Carpenter of Massachusetts designed and stitched a true labor of love in a needlework created for her granddaughter, Leah C. Carpenter. Basic embroidery stitches were used in this detail. Photo by Richard Carpenter.

Here are some tips:

- Scatter your stitching rather than beginning in one place and continuing from there. Then, one area will not stand out if your stitching changes. The same technique can be used to distribute a thread color over a quilt top.

- To make your stitching more even, establish a rhythm as you work. However, uneven stitching can be more interesting to look at!

- Don't be afraid to rip them out if you don't like your stitches.

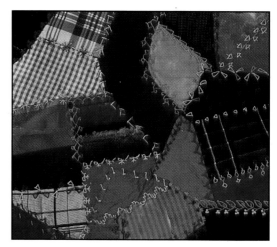

Note the unusual stitches on this antique crazy quilt block! Collection of Rocky Mountain Quilts, York Village, Maine.

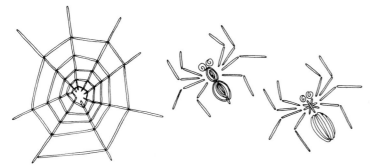

Spiders and Webs

Spiders and webs often appear on antique crazy quilts, along with other common motifs such as fans and rings.

There are many theories regarding the use of spiders and webs in quilting and the needle arts. Crazy quilting was very popular in its day, and the "symbols" appearing on quilts may be simply the embroidery subjects of the time. We can ascribe our own meanings if we wish to do so. For myself, I think that nature weaves an intricate web, and we are part of that intricacy—patches in the web of life!

It only stands to reason that spiders can be portrayed in as many ways as there are types of them, and there are many. For starters, spiders are shiny or dull, short- or long-legged, small or large, colorful or gray, patterned or plain, luminescent or hairy. Some have eight eyes, others have none. They all have eight legs!

The same goes for webs. Not all are perfectly shaped.

To embroider a web, couch metallic, rayon, or silk threads making the long strands, then fill in the shorter ones.

A spider can be made of embroidery stitches, or by combining several sizes of beads.

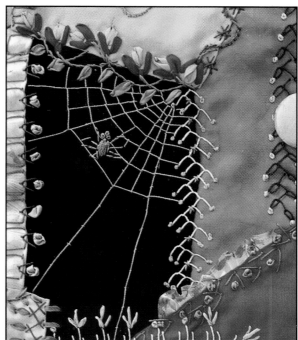

Spiders and spider webs are favorite subjects for embroidery on crazy quilts, as here on the Ladies and Fans quilt.

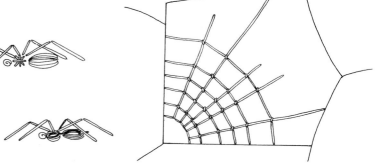

Embroidery Stitches

Almost all of the stitches are begun by bringing the thread up through after having fastened it onto the back of the fabric. So, this part of the instruction is assumed, and not given.

Left-handed diagrams are provided for most of the stitches. Where not given, it should be easy enough to follow the diagrams:

Reverse any "to the right" instructions to read "to the left," and vice versa.

Blanket Stitch and Related Stitches

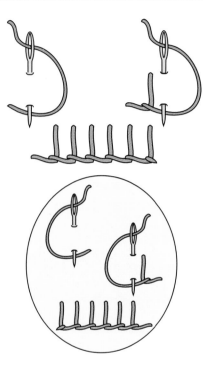

Blanket stitching secures heart-shaped appliqués in addition to patch-seam embroidery.

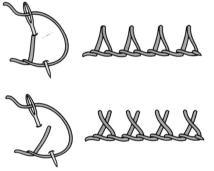

Blanket stitch—this stitch can be made in either direction—toward the left or the right. Stitch vertically, having the thread under the needle. Pull through and repeat. End with a short tacking stitch.

Buttonhole stitch—work the same as blanket stitch, making the stitches very close together.

Blanket fan—work the same as blanket stitch, but use the same hole in the fabric for the beginning of each stitch, making as many stitches as needed. Finish with a straight stitch.

Closed or crossed buttonhole—slant the upper parts of the stitch together in pairs, meeting at the top for closed, and overlapping for crossed buttonhole.

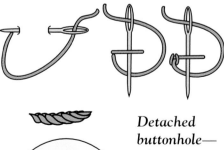

Detached buttonhole—make a straight stitch, then work buttonhole onto it without piercing the fabric. One detached button-

hole makes a delicate leaf; work several in a circle to form a rose.

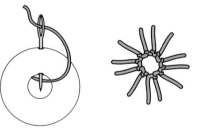

Eyelet—draw a small circle inside a larger one on the fabric. Work buttonhole stitch around.

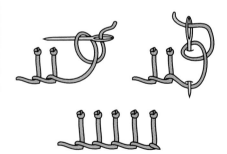

Knotted buttonhole—following the diagram, wrap the thread once. Pull tight and then finish the stitch.

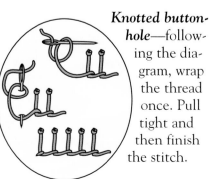

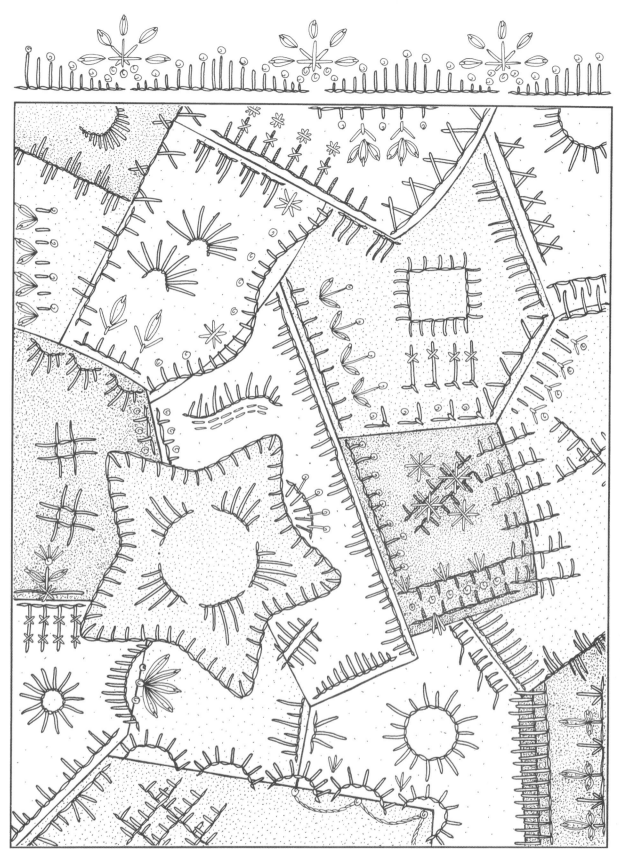

Blanket Stitch Variations & Combinations

Other needlework: Blanket stitch is used to edge wool blankets and clothing, and to apply appliqués. The Buttonhole stitch is used for buttonholes, appliqué, monogramming, and other fine embroidery.

Bullion Knot and Related Stitches

The bullion stitch lends itself well to wool embroidery, as here on the Horses and Roses quilt.

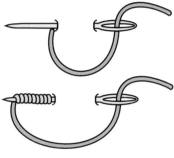

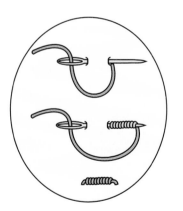

Bullion knot—it may take a few tries to learn these, but is worth doing. Make a stitch but do not pull through. Wrap the end of the needle evenly enough times to equal the distance of the stitch. Hold the wraps in place while pulling the needle through. Sink the needle where the stitch began, then give a little tug to settle the wraps in place.

Bullion rose—begin with three short bullion knots placed in a triangle. Surround them with longer bullions in a circular fashion.

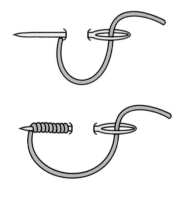

Looped bullion—same as the bullion knot, but make the wrapped part of the stitch at least twice as long as the original stitch.

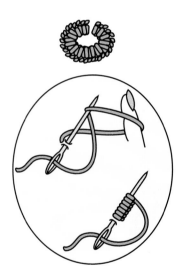

Cast-on stitch—first, make a small stitch and do not pull through. Following the diagram, wrap the yarn around your finger as shown, then pick it up with the needle. Slide the stitch onto the needle and then repeat to make an even row of stitches on the needle. Pull the needle through the stitches. Sink it close to the first stitch. The size of the finished stitch will depend on the number of cast-on stitches.

Bullion Knot Variations & Combinations

Other needlework: Bullion knots are used in dimensional embroidery, especially wool, and Brazilian embroidery, which is worked in rayon threads. Try them in silk ribbon!

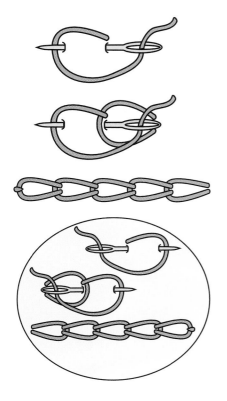

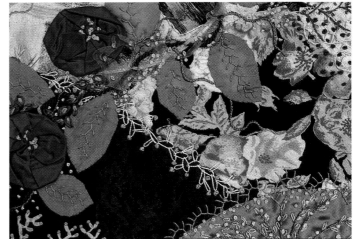

The chain stitch and variations of it form an excellent base for additional stitches as demonstrated on the Piano Shawl.

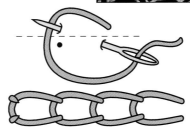

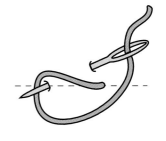

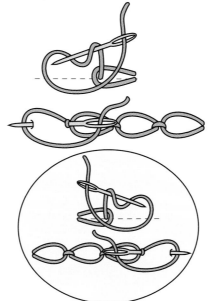

Chain stitch—make this stitch in either direction—toward the left or the right. Stitch horizontally having the thread under the needle. Pull through and repeat. End with a short tacking stitch.

Chain stitch rose—beginning at the center, work chain stitch in a circular fashion until the rose is the size desired.

Magic chain—thread the needle with two different colors or types of thread. Working the chain stitch, separate the two threads and use one of them to make the first stitch, then the other for the following stitch. Repeat.

Open chain—begin the stitch following the direction of the needle as shown. Begin the next stitch at the dot, and repeat. End with two tacking stitches.

Cable chain—make one chain stitch, wrap the thread once around the needle, pull snug, and make the following chain stitch not into the first stitch, but just past it.

Twisted chain—follow the diagram, and repeat as shown. End with a tacking stitch.

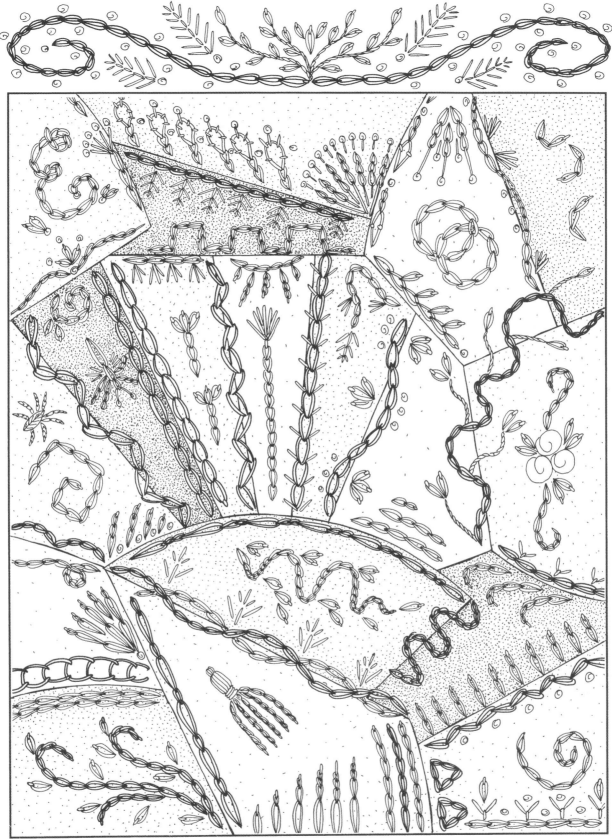

Chain Stitch Variations & Combinations

Other needlework: Very fine chain stitch worked evenly to form various designs is called "tambour work" which is often done using a hook. This is worked on net or sheer fabric for a lacey effect, or to attach beads. Some very beautiful tambour work was done in the late 1700s and early 1800s in the U.S. and Europe to make baby's caps, shawls, collars, and bridal veils. The chain stitch is also used for outlining and filler in crewel and other types of embroidery.

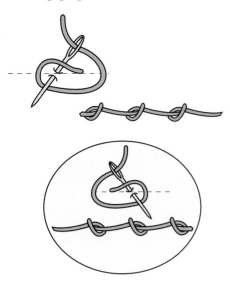

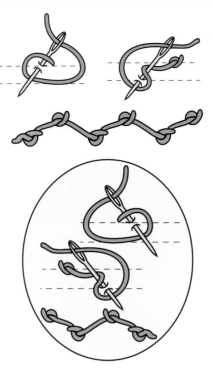

The zigzag coral stitch on the Ladies and Fans quilt.

Coral stitch—make a short slanted stitch, having the thread go over and then under the needle. Keep the thread snug while pulling through. Repeat, working toward the left. The stitch can be worked from left to right by wrapping the thread in the opposite direction.

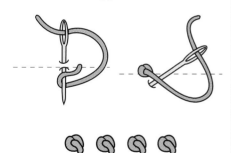

Coral knot—make a coral stitch vertically, then finish with a tacking stitch. Make these in a row or scatter them.

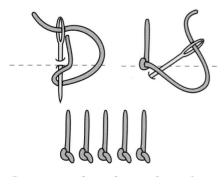

Long-armed single coral stitch—make these in rows or individually. Make the same as the coral knot, but take a longer stitch.

Zigzag coral stitch—make a coral stitch at the top of the row. Wrap the thread over the needle, and then make a second coral stitch at the bottom of the row, wrapping the thread in the opposite direction. Repeat.

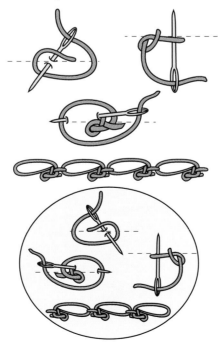

Knotted cable chain stitch—this is a combination of coral, lacing, and chain stitch. Make a coral stitch, pass the needle up through

without piercing the fabric and then make a chain stitch. Repeat.

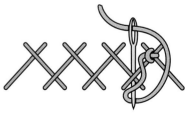

Coral knotted herringbone—first, make a row of herringbone stitches. Fasten on a second thread, and work zigzag coral stitch over the crossed parts of the herringbone without piercing the fabric.

Coral Stitch Variations & Combinations

Other needlework: Excellent in landscape embroideries, the main feature of this stitch is its textural quality. Try it in different thread types and in silk ribbon. Use this stitch to couch other threads.

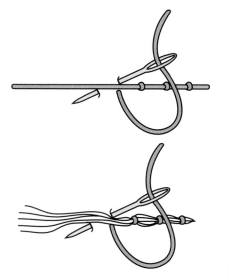

Couching with French knots and buttons holds ribbons in place on the Victorian quilt.

Couching—fasten on the thread or fiber to be couched, or secure its ends under patch seams. With a second thread, stitch over the couched thread and through the fabric. Use short tacking stitches.

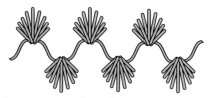

Using an embroidery stitch—use an embroidery stitch to secure the couched fiber. Among the stitches that work well are blanket fan, French knot, lazy daisy, fly, and etc.

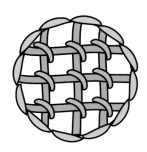

Filler couching—fill an area with long stitches and then couch them at intervals to hold them in place.

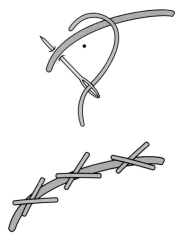

Thorn stitch—make a long stitch of a heavy thread, shaping it into a curve. With a second thread make cross stitches over the heavy thread to secure it in place.

Sheaf stitch—make three vertical straight stitches, then bring them together with a short tacking stitch in the middle.

A mix of textures and details are shown in this detail of the Landscape hanging.

Couching Variations & Combinations

Other needlework: Couching was often worked on Victorian crazy quilts to fasten on chenille or stranded threads. In Brazilian embroidery, it is used to form fine leaves and branches. In silk and metal embroideries, couching secures metal threads that cannot be sewn through fabric, and in silk ribbon embroidery to fasten laid ribbons.

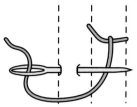

The Cretan stitch makes an elegant row along patch seams on the Ladies and Fans quilt.

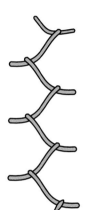

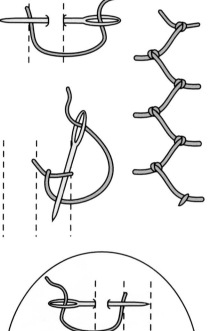

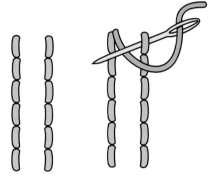

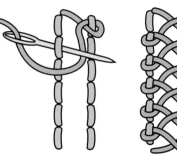

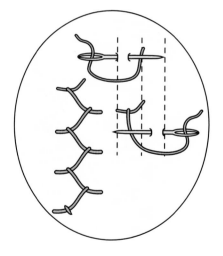

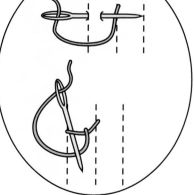

Raised cretan—work two rows of backstitches evenly. Without piercing the fabric, work the cretan stitch between them.

Cretan stitch—work downward, keeping the needle horizontal. With the thread under the needle, first make a stitch at the right of an imaginary line then a stitch at the left. Repeat. The stitch can be worked closely or spread apart.

Knotted cretan stitch—begin the cretan stitch as shown. Then, pass the needle under the stitch just made and pull snug. Repeat.

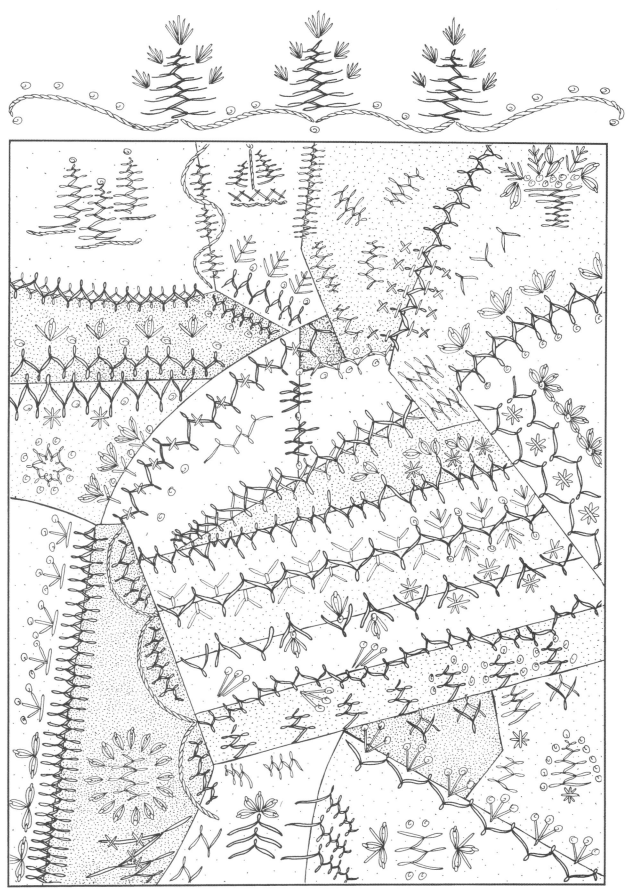

Cretan Stitch Variations & Combinations

Other needlework: The cretan stitch is used to form leaves in crewel and other forms of embroidery. The open cretan is an extremely versatile crazy quilting stitch, quick to make, and easily embellished with additional stitches.

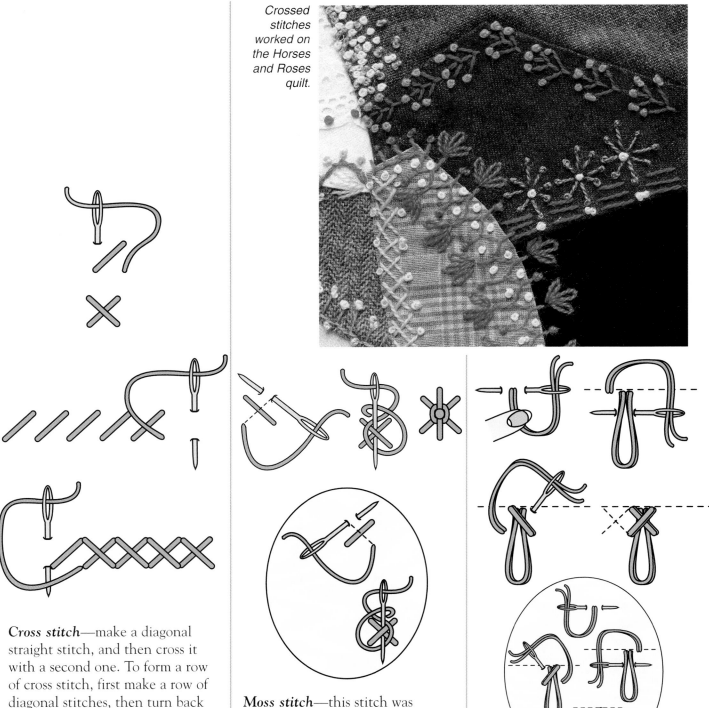

Crossed stitches worked on the Horses and Roses quilt.

Cross stitch—make a diagonal straight stitch, and then cross it with a second one. To form a row of cross stitch, first make a row of diagonal stitches, then turn back and cross each stitch.

Star stitch—make one cross stitch on top of another. A small tacking stitch can be added at the center.

Moss stitch—this stitch was invented by Marion Nichols, author of *Encyclopedia of Embroidery Stitches* (see Bibliography). Make a cross stitch, bringing the needle up above the stitch as shown. Form a loop, then place the needle over the loop and through the cross stitch without piercing the fabric. Pull through and sink the needle below the stitch.

Victorian fringe stitch—using a doubled thread, follow the diagrams to form a loop. Holding the loop in place, form a crossed stitch at the upper part of the loop. Repeat, sharing the holes of the previous stitch to make the next.

Cross Stitch Variations & Combinations

Other needlework: Cross stitch is a common form of embroidery worked on Aida cloth or evenweave linen. Small star stitches appear as small dots and are used as filler stitches in crewel embroidery. The half cross stitch is useful for sewing on beads.

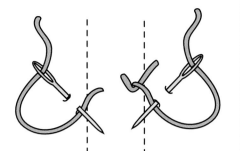

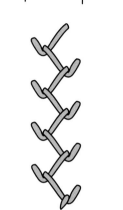

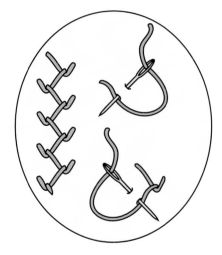

Feather stitch—working downward along an imaginary line, make a slanting stitch first to one side of the line then the other. Repeat.

Stacked feather stitch—make the feather stitch in the shape of a leaf, working the stitches close together.

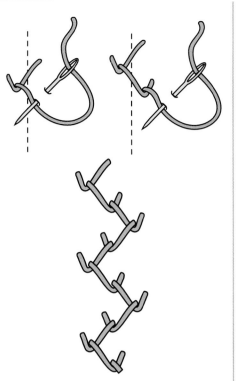

Double feather stitch—work the same as the feather stitch, but make an extra stitch at each side of the line.

The double feather stitch is an interesting seam treatment.

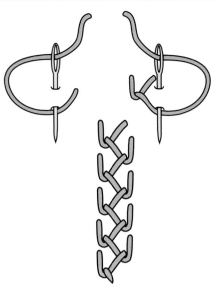

Straight-sided feather stitch—make the same as the feather stitch, but with vertical "arms."

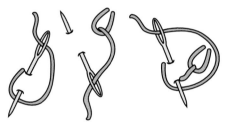

Chained feather stitch—this consists of long-stemmed lazy daisy stitches placed in the same formation as a feather stitch. Follow the diagrams.

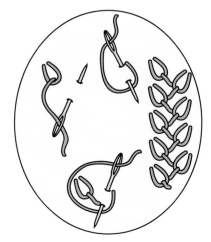

Feather Stitch Variations & Combinations

Other needlework: The feather stitch is a beautiful stitch and is used in many antique crazy quilts, sometimes as the only decorative stitch. This stitch was known as "coral stitch" or "brier stitch" in Victorian times. The Victorian "feather stitch" resembled a slanted blanket stitch.

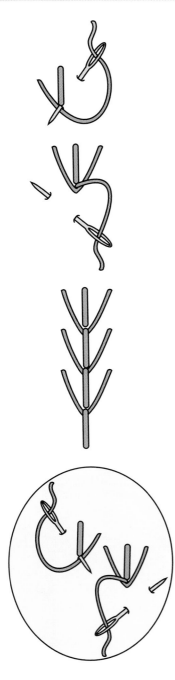

Fern stitch surrounds an appliqué on the Butterstamp quilt.

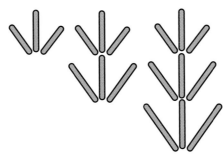

Straight stitch fern—the second way to form the stitch is to arrange straight stitches in groups of three.

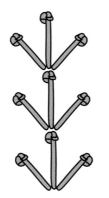

Pistil fern—arrange pistil stitches (see page 56) in groups of three.

Fern stitch—there are two ways to form this stitch. One is to begin with a straight stitch followed by fly stitches.

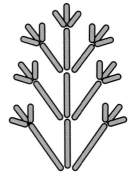

Multi-branched fern—make the straight stitch fern. Then add groups of three shorter stitches to the ends of "branches."

Fern Stitch Variations & Combinations

Other needlework: This stitch can easily be worked to fit the "grid" of evenweave fabric in cross stitch or needlepoint designs. In silk ribbon embroidery, twist the ribbon to make ferns.

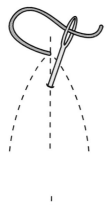

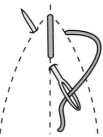

Excellent for leaves, the closed fishbone stitch surrounds wool roses on the Horses and Roses quilt.

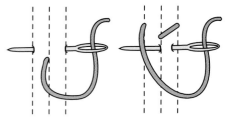

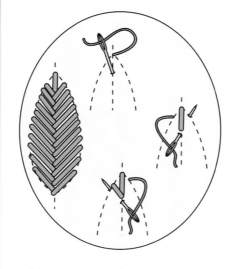

Fishbone stitch—begin with a vertical straight stitch. Then make diagonal stitches following the diagram. The stitches will overlap slightly at the center. Draw, or follow an imaginary leaf shape.

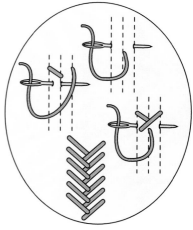

Open fishbone—draw, or follow three imaginary lines on the fabric. Stitch as shown in the diagram, repeating the sequence.

Fishbone Variations & Combinations

Other needlework: The fishbone stitch defies exact definition. There are several different ways to make the stitch. It can be used to form leaves in wool, crewel, and other types of embroidery.

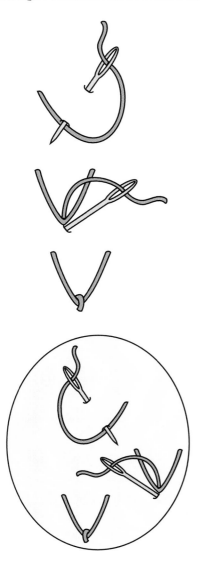

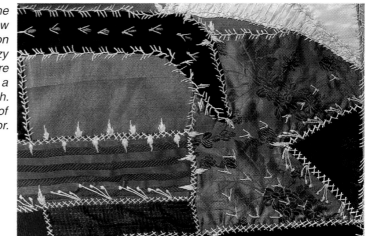

Fly stitch is one of only a few stitch types on this 1898 Crazy quilt. These are scattered on a patch. Collection of the author.

Fly stitch—with the thread under the needle, make a diagonal stitch as shown. End with a short tacking stitch.

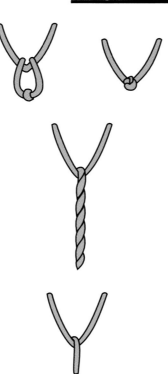

Fly variations—tack the stitch using a straight stitch, French knot, lazy daisy, or outline stitch.

Stacked fly—make a series of fly stitches vertically.

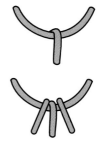

Crown stitch—make a wide, shallow long-stemmed fly, then add two straight stitches.

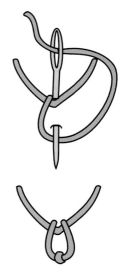

Tete de Boeuf—this consists of a fly stitch tacked with a lazy daisy. The name means "head of the bull." The stitch is sometimes called "wheat-ear."

Fly Stitch Variations & Combinations

Other needlework: Among the uses for fly stitch include its versatility in building up stitch combinations, and its use as a base for a flower or bud. Scatter them for filler stitches.

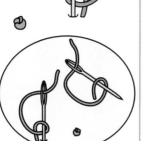

French knot—wrap the thread around the needle as shown, pull snug, and pull through close to where the stitch began. Vary the stitch by wrapping two or three times around the needle, and/or keep the wraps loose before pulling through.

Pistil stitch—make the same as the French knot, but sink the needle farther away.

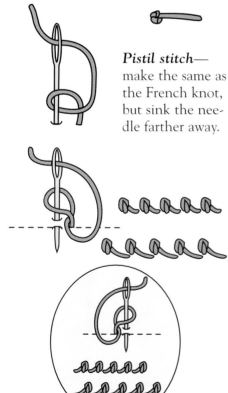

Continuous French knot—make the same as the French knot, but end by making a short stitch, then repeat. Place the stitches farther apart to make the continuous pistil stitch.

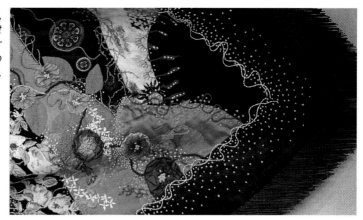

A favorite stitch, the French knot adds character to the Piano Shawl.

Italian knotted border stitch—this stitch consists of an elongated fly stitch that is tacked with a French knot. It can be worked in either direction—left or right.

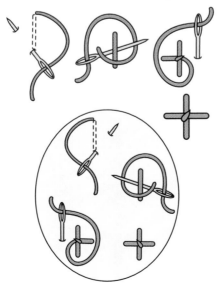

Four-legged knot stitch—this stitch combines a cross stitch with a French knot. Follow the dia-

grams, knotting the stitch by sliding the needle under the previous stitch without piercing the fabric. Form a loop, and pull snug, then finish the cross stitch.

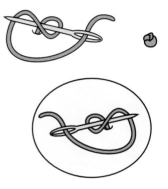

Colonial knot—follow the direction of the thread in the diagram, wrapping the thread under, then over the needle in a figure 8 configuration. Snug up the thread, and then pull through near to the beginning of the stitch.

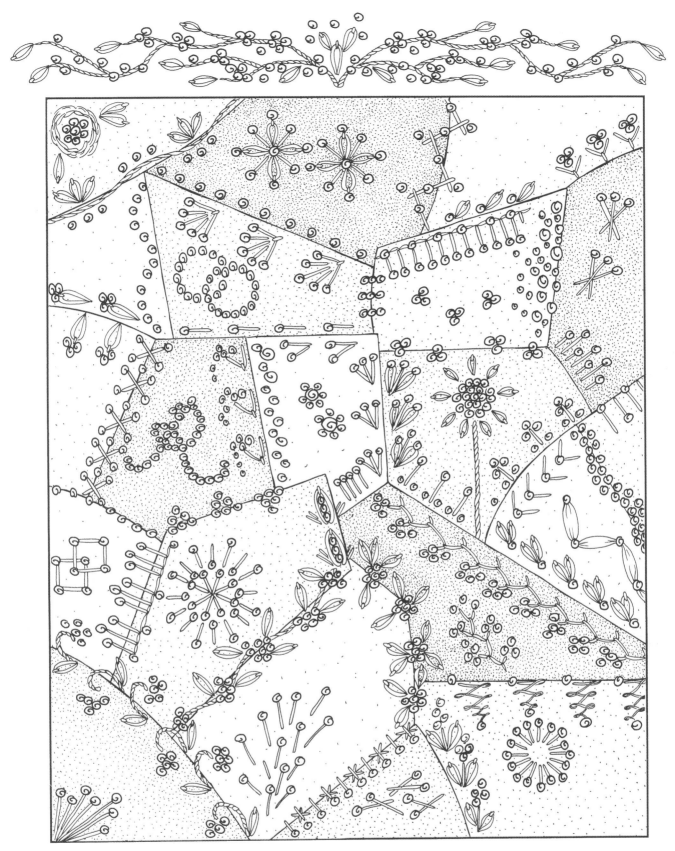

French Knot Variations & Combinations

Other needlework: The French knot is used as a filler stitch in crewel and other embroidery, and sometimes in place of the colonial knot for candlewicking. It can be added to needlepoint or cross stitch. The pistil stitch is useful in embroidering flowers.

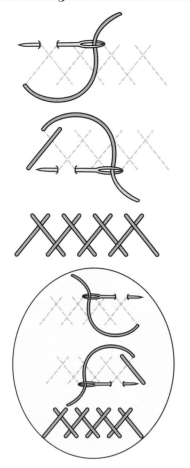

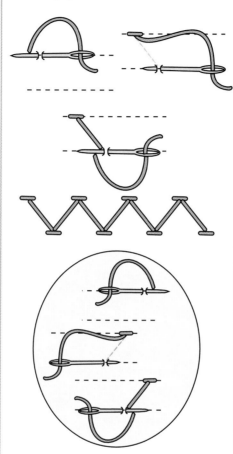

the previous stitches. Another way to achieve the same effect is to make a row of regular herringbone stitches, then a second row to fill in the gaps.

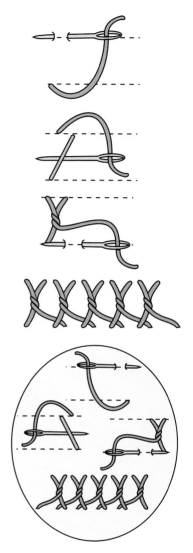

the stitch are formed by small backstitches.

Herringbone stitch—working toward the right, make one stitch at the top of the row keeping the thread below the needle. Make the next stitch at the bottom of the row with the thread above the needle. The needle faces previously made stitches.

Chevron stitch—follow the steps shown in the diagram, and repeat. The bars at the top and bottom of

Breton stitch—make a slanting stitch (same as beginning the herringbone), then wrap the thread around the stitch without piercing the fabric, and finish as shown. Repeat.

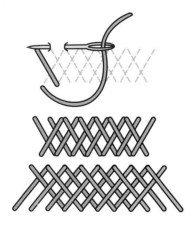

Closed herringbone—make the same as the herringbone, but place the stitches closely so that new stitches share the holes made by

The herringbone stitch is commonly seen on antique crazy quilts. Collection of the author.

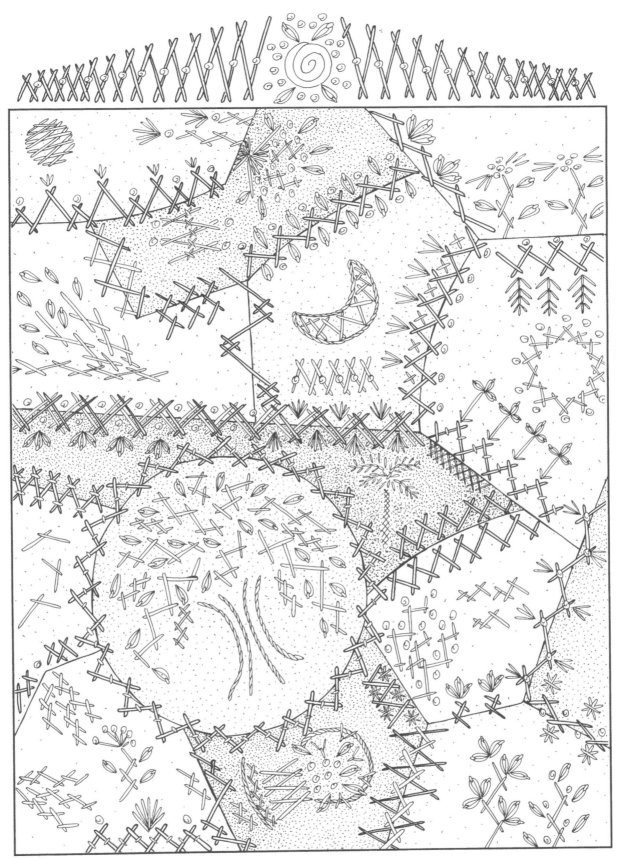

Herringbone Stitch Variations & Combinations

Other needlework: The herringbone and related stitches are excellent for a base row along crazy quilt patch seams. The chevron stitch is commonly used for smocking.

Lazy Daisy Stitch and Related Stitches

Lazy daisies almost always seem to have "flower appeal" including here on the Butterstamp quilt.

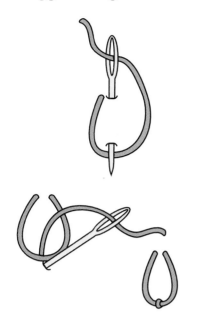

Lazy daisy stitch—make the stitch as shown having the thread under the needle, and pull through. End with a short tacking stitch.

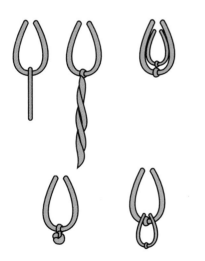

Lazy daisy variations—tack the stitch using a straight stitch, French knot, lazy daisy, or outline stitch.

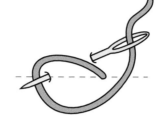

Detached twisted chain stitch—follow the diagram, stitching in a diagonal direction and having the thread go under the needle. End with a short tacking stitch.

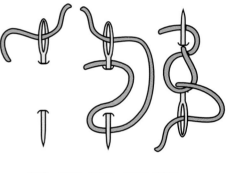

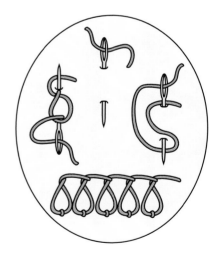

Basque stitch—begin the stitch, but do not pull through. Wrap the thread in an "S" shape around the needle, pull snug, then pull through. Then, insert the needle beneath the stitch and coming out at the top of it, pull through. Repeat from the beginning, working towards the right.

Lazy Daisy Stitch Variations & Combinations

Other needlework: This stitch is a single version of the chain stitch, and is sometimes called "single chain," or "detached chain." The Victorians termed it the "picot stitch." The stitch has many uses, from delineating flower petals, to filler stitches in crewel and other embroideries. It can be worked on top of needlepoint for added dimension, and in cross stitch. The lazy daisy stitch is very useful in silk ribbon embroidery to form flowers of many types.

Outline Stitch and Related Stitches

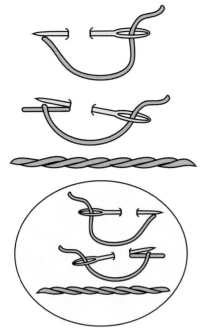

Kate Greenaway's drawings of children appear in outline stitch on many antique crazy quilts. The embroideries on the Cousins quilt are from iron-on transfers published by Dover Publications, Inc. (see Sources).

Outline stitch—stitch toward the right having the needle facing left. Stitches can be made immediately next to each other as shown, or they can be overlapped slightly to make a heavier line, or farther apart for a narrower line.

Overcast outline—work the outline stitch, and fasten off. Fasten on a second thread, and overcast by sliding the needle under each stitch without piercing the fabric.

Split stitch—work the same as the backstitch, but working into the previous stitch. This stitch makes a very fine outline.

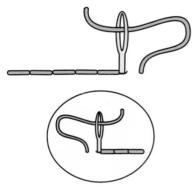

Backstitch—bring the needle up a stitch length ahead of the previous stitch, and back down in the same hole as the previous stitch. (The reverse of the stitch appears the same as the outline stitch).

Outline stitch rose— beginning at the center, make outline stitches in a circular fashion. Begin the stitches very short, and make them longer as you progress. End when the rose is as large as you like it.

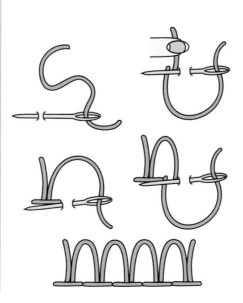

Above is an innovative use of the outline stitch on an 1898 crazy quilt. Detail. Collection of the author.

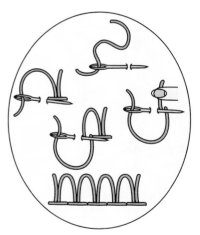

Turkey work—do not fasten the thread to the back of the fabric. Make a short stitch, pull through and hold the thread end with your thumb. Make a short stitch having the thread under the needle. Continue as shown. The loops can be trimmed if desired.

Outline Stitch Variations & Combinations

Other needlework: Also called "stem stitch," the outline is used in outlining designs that are not filled in, as well as in those that are. "Redwork" is a type of embroidery in which designs are outlined in red embroidery thread, and left unfilled. Outline stitch roses are used in wool or silk ribbon embroidery.

Useful in Landscape quilting, the running stitch can be like painting with thread as shown on this detail of the Landscape Hanging.

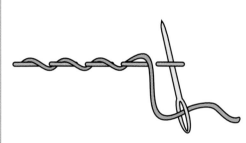

Overcast running stitch—work the running stitch, and fasten off. Fasten on a second thread, and overcast by sliding the needle under each stitch without piercing the fabric.

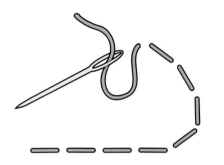

Running stitch—make a line of even stitches, making one at a time, or with several on the needle before pulling through.

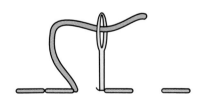

Holbein stitch—make a row of running stitches and fasten off. At the end of the row, fasten on a second thread and make a return row of running stitches filling in the spaces left previously.

Interlaced running stitch—lace the stitches as shown first with one thread, then filling in with a second thread.

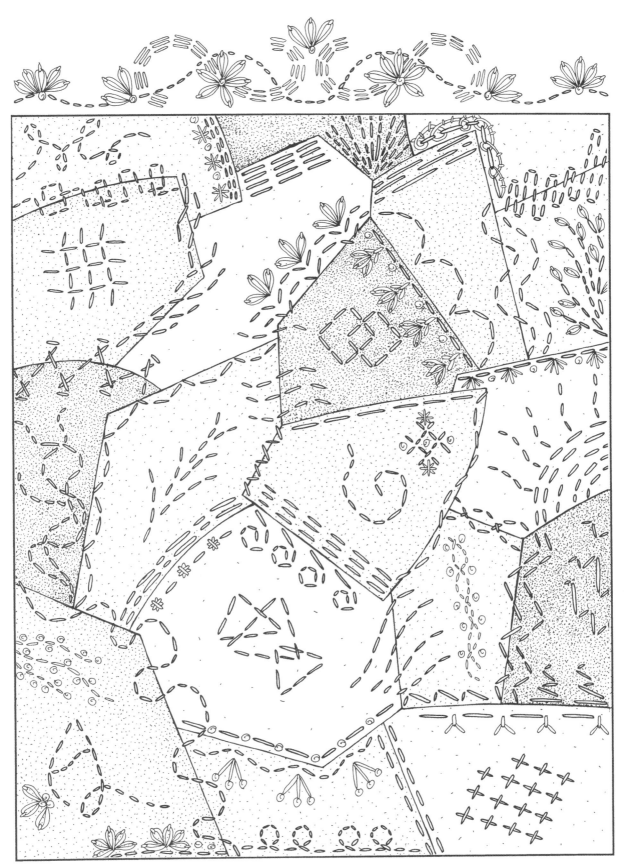

Running Stitch Variations & Combinations

Other needlework: Made tiny and evenly, this is the quilting stitch. It is also used for sashiko, Oriental quilting that is worked in a white thread, such as size 8 pearl cotton, usually on one layer of indigo-blue fabric to reinforce the fabric, rather than quilt layers together. The holbein stitch is used in blackwork.

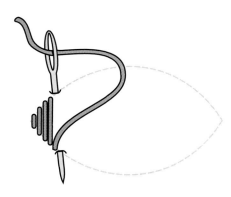

Satin stitch—fill an area by stitching from one side to the other, having the stitches immediately next to each other. To ensure a neat edge, first outline the area in backstitch or outline stitch, then work satin stitch over the outlining.

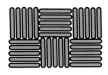

Basket satin—make groups of satin stitch perpendicular to each other.

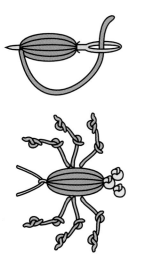

Beetle stitch—work the satin stitch repeatedly between the same two holes in the fabric, until the stitches mound up. Add eyes of French knots, legs of straight stitch, and antennae of pistil stitch.

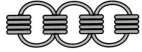

Laced satin stitch—work a row of small satin stitches and then, without piercing the fabric, lace between.

Long and short stitch—work satin stitch alternating long with short stitches. Use this to fill in larger areas and to shade designs.

Satin stitch embroideries make excellent patch decorations. This embroidery is worked from Dover Publications' Traditional Chinese Designs, by Barbara Christopher (see Sources).

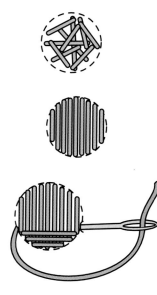

Padded satin stitch—begin by filling in the design with one or more layers of straight or other stitches. These can also be worked over a small amount of batting for extra loft. Finish with satin stitch to completely cover the padding. Satin stitch can be worked first in one direction, then the other for extra coverage.

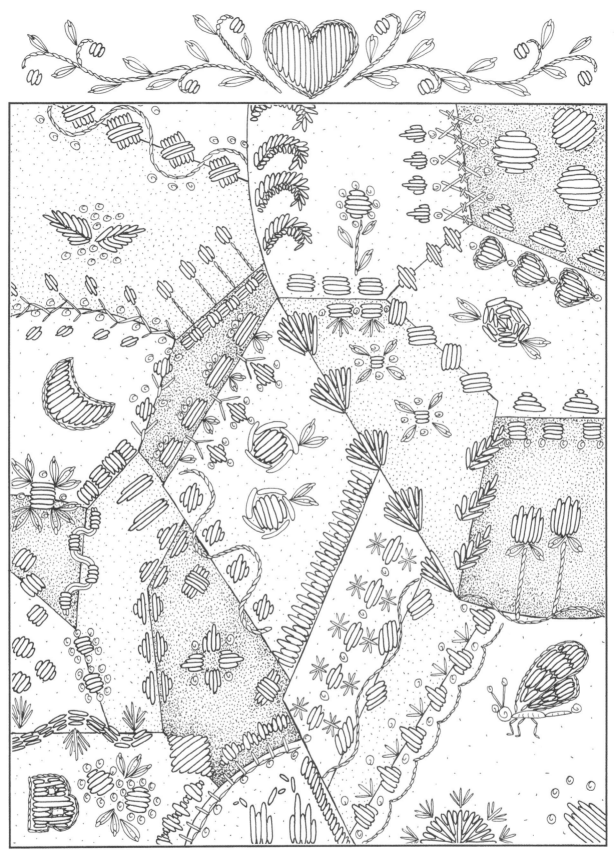

Satin Stitch Variations & Combinations

Other needlework: Coming from many different embroidery traditions, from most parts of the world, satin stitch embroidery is perhaps best known by beautiful and colorful Oriental embroideries worked in lustrous silk threads. Monograms stitched in cotton floss are a Western tradition, with many elaborate ones done by the Victorians.

Square and "V" and Related Stitches

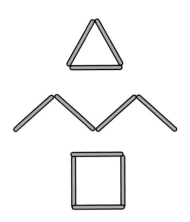

Square and "V" stitches are created using straight and other stitches. There are many variations of these on antique crazy quilts. Collection of the author.

Square and "V" stitches—Form angles, triangles, squares and rectangles out of straight stitches.

Tied straight stitches.

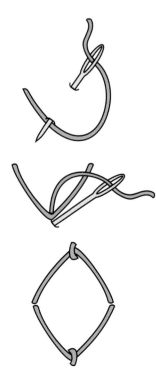

Fly variation—make square shapes out of large fly stitches.

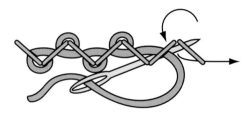

Four-sided stitch—use straight or backstitches to make squares and rectangles.

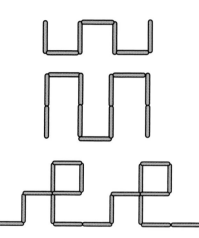

Rice stitch—work a row of large cross stitches, then a following row of stitches that cross the cross stitches.

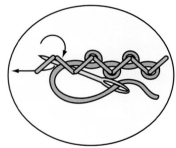

Threaded arrow stitch—make a row of "V" stitches. Follow it with a row of lacing without piercing the fabric. The arrows show the placement of the following lacing stitch.

Square and "V" Variations & Combinations

Other needlework: These are not stitches as such. They are formed of other stitches such as straight, fly, and sometimes blanket stitch. Generally, they are made larger and more emphatically than regular stitches, and parts of them are sometimes "tied" with tacking stitches. Found on antique crazy quilts, they may have been an attempt to invent stitches.

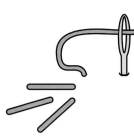

Straight stitch—bring the needle up, then down through the fabric. Make stitches any size, placed evenly or randomly.

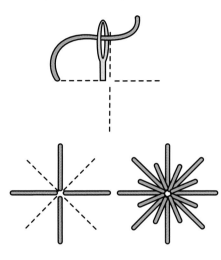

Algerian eye stitch—having all stitches converge at the center, make four stitches vertically and horizontally, then four diagonally. Add shorter stitches between the longer ones.

Seed stitch—place two small stitches side-by-side, and repeat.

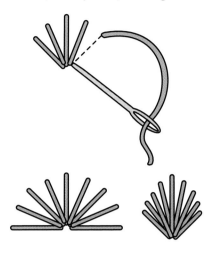

Straight stitch fan—all stitches begin at the top and converge at the base. Make fans rounded, tapered, or widened. Use as many stitches as desired.

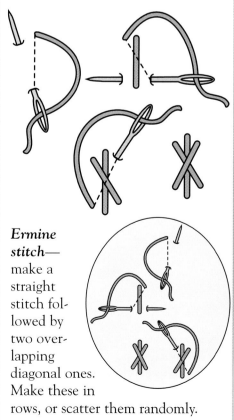

Ermine stitch—make a straight stitch followed by two overlapping diagonal ones. Make these in rows, or scatter them randomly.

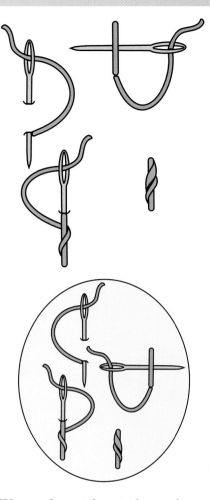

Wrapped straight stitch—make a straight stitch, then pass the needle under it without piercing the fabric. Sink the needle at the top of the stitch.

The simplest of stitches, the straight stitch has many variations as seen on this antique crazy quilt block. Collection of the author.

Straight Stitch Variations & Combinations

Other needlework: One of the most versatile of all stitches, the straight stitch can be used to form the fern stitch, box, and "V," and fan stitches. Putting a French knot at one end simulates the pistil stitch. These are found on many Victorian crazy quilts, and as filler stitches in crewel and other embroideries. The Algerian eye stitch is traditionally found in needlepoint and cross stitch designs.

Begin by making the base stitches. Fasten on a second thread and lace or weave through them. This thread does not pierce the fabric except to begin and end.

Woven roses and fans worked in wool threads on the Horses and Roses quilt.

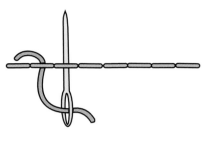

Double-laced backstitch—work a row of backstitch. Fasten on a second thread and lace through the stitches without piercing the fabric. Work a second row in the reverse direction.

Woven satin stitch—fill an area with satin stitch. Fasten on a second thread and weave back and forth until it is filled in.

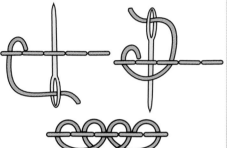

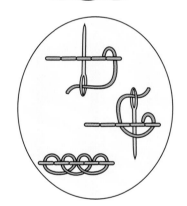

Pekinese stitch—work a row of backstitches. Fasten on a second thread as shown and pass the needle under the first stitch. Skip one stitch and bring the needle up under the next. Go down through the skipped stitch, and repeat.

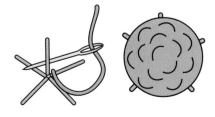

Woven rose—make an odd number of spokes out of straight stitches. Fasten on a second thread and weave around until filled in.

Raised spider web—make any number of spokes out of straight stitches. Fasten on a second thread, and work a backstitch over one spoke and under the previous two. Repeat, working clockwise.

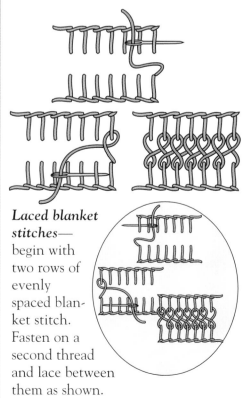

Laced blanket stitches—begin with two rows of evenly spaced blanket stitch. Fasten on a second thread and lace between them as shown.

Woven and Laced Stitch Variations & Combinations

Other needlework: Woven roses are common to wool and silk ribbon embroidery.

Chapter 3

Artful Embellishments

It is their artful embellishments that distinguish the most fanciful of crazy quilts. Satin-stitched monograms interlaced with embroidered flowers, charming Kate Greenaway outlined figures, ribbons fashioned into flowers, and sewn-on beads, buttons, and tassels are some examples. Other ways to embellish include painting, stenciling, and transferring photos onto fabric. In addition to the fancy stitches worked along patch edges, embellishments add dimension, color, texture, and variety to the "crazed china" surface of crazy patching. All of these additions enliven a quilt by taking its surface beyond the ordinary, explaining why crazy quilts are sometimes referred to as "art quilts."

This showpiece crazy quilt features floral paintings and embroideries. Collection of Rocky Mountain Quilts, York Village, Maine.

Like works of art, from simple to complex, a crazy quilt is the unique expression of its maker. Sometimes it doesn't take much. Simple techniques can be extraordinary in their effect, from fastening on an old piece of lace with a particular embroidery stitch, to discovering a fabulous new way to sew a scrap of fabric into the shape of a flower.

The individual touches that each pair of hands, like handwriting, bring to a quilt-in-progress are enough to put a stamp of personality on it.

Try the techniques in this chapter, experimenting on scraps of fabric and saving them to use as patches. Is it backwards to embellish the patches before patching the quilt? Not at all! While you are at it, check to see if you have pieces of unfinished needlework hidden away in a closet or the attic. Unfinished pieces can often find new life on a crazy quilt.

Adding Antiques

Poking around in antiques shops can turn up some interesting trinkets to add to crazy quilt projects. Clothing and other textiles in worn condition can sometimes be salvaged for their still-good parts. (Pieces that are whole should not be cut up.) Some dealers sell laces and trims that have been removed from clothing and linens. Hats, belts, and gloves and fabric purses may have parts worth using, and many types of doilies are commonly found.

Cigarette Silks

Cigarette silks were used as premiums in cigarette packages. In the early 1900s, cigarette advertising became highly competitive, and although it was not quite acceptable for women to smoke, they played a large role in sales of cigarettes. You can likely imagine a woman fond of needlework egging her husband to buy a pack of ciggies so she can have the silk! The manufacturers of cigarettes went so far as to print suggestions for needlework projects using the silks including table covers, doilies, portieres, and clothing accessories.

There were several types of "silks" made. One manufacturer referred to the smaller ones shown here as "satin wonders." Close examination of these reveals a heavy base thread that appears to be cotton beneath a silk satin outer surface. The satin surface was printed by a process called chromolithography, capable of hairline details in depicting women, flags, birds, butterflies, flowers, and other subject matter.

Another premium was the "felt," a piece of cotton flannel fabric printed with an image. Many of these were flags, but butterflies and other designs can also be found. These were larger than the silks, and they had to be specially mail ordered.

The silks and felts are now quite delicate and should be handled carefully. Do not turn their edges under. To fasten them onto quilts, lay ribbons over their edges and lightly embroider or tack the ribbons. Fasten them on in the final stages of making the quilt top, and do not sew them onto quilts that will receive active wear.

Antiques awaiting a crazy quilt project include buttons, cigarette silks and felts, hankie, doily, and crocheted laces.

Laces

Laces of many types can be found in antiques shops. If you are going to cut them up, find pieces that are beyond repair, in which sections are still useable. (Also consider making your own laces—knitted, crocheted, tatted, or bobbin or tape lace.)

Hankies

Victorian ladies carried silk hankies. A pretty, whole one in good condition can be tacked onto a central patch on a crazy quilt. Use pieces of salvaged ones as patches.

Buttons

Antique buttons can sometimes be found in reasonably priced jarfuls, and this is the way to buy them. You will doubtless find a place for each one on your projects!

Needlework

Old needlework in good condition, such as crewel, needlepoint, and other types, can often be used as patches. Use full-size pieces as quilt centers. Unfinished pieces that are likely not to be finished can be cut up and appliquéd or used as patches. If the design seems outdated, try adding ribbonwork or silk ribbon embroidery to them.

Creating Moments

The beauty of a fancy crazy quilt is in its details—those areas that attract the eye of the viewer. I call it "creating a moment" when I am working on one of these areas, a moment being the amount of time it seems to take when you are entranced by working on something. From the viewer's perspective, a small area of beauty catches the eye for a moment.

It is easy to create a "moment" of your own. Place a 14" lap hoop onto a selected area of the quilt (and leave it there until finished). Appliqué a fabric photo, sew on a cluster of ribbonwork flowers, or a lace motif. Add to it with couched ribbons, silk ribbon or other embroidery and then add some beads or buttons. Continue to add until the area seems complete, a mini work of art.

Remember to be kind to yourself. When doing needlework, I often find myself so entranced that I forget to notice aches. It is important to remember to stand up and move around and stretch. Good circulation sparks creativity! Oops, an ouch can be too late! Bigger damage spells the fate.

Small areas of intricate detail draw the eye of the viewer. Detail of the Ladies and Fans quilt.

A needlepoint design by Anne Orr, from Full-Color Charted Designs, published by Dover Publications, Inc., 1984. Anne Orr created needlework designs in the early 1900s. The design shown is stitched of silk ribbons, wool, silk, and rayon threads and then used as a patch on the Horses and Roses quilt.

Materials
Fabric scraps

Size 12 Sharp needle

Silk pins

Size 50 cotton or silk sewing thread

Beeswax

Dry iron and spray bottle

Scissors

Appliqué is sewing one fabric onto another. Use it to add an area of color such as a bowl or basket shape and then fill it with embroidered flowers. Choose light to medium-weight fabrics that hold a crease and are not prone to fraying. Tightly woven cottons, silks, rayon or wool challis, and taffeta are some examples. Stick with bold, squared, or rounded shapes, since intricate shapes tend to lose detail in the process of sewing them on.

Instructions
1. Cut out the shape, adding a ⅛" to ¼" seam allowance. Clip curves almost to the seam allowance if need be. Press the seam allowance under. Pin or baste the appliqué to the ground fabric. Note: an appliqué can be sewn without pressing first. Use the tip of the needle to turn the edge under before each stitch.
2. Slipstitch, using a matching or blending thread color. Use 100 percent cotton, or silk, size 50 thread. Run the thread over beeswax to deter tangles.
3. To slipstitch, run the needle through the fold of the pressed edge of the appliqué and then pick up a thread or two of the ground fabric. Keep the stitches short and invisible.
4. Embroider any details.

A piece of an unfinished crewel embroidery appliquéd on the Horses and Roses quilt.

This appliquéd and embroidered design is reminiscent of Victorian era embroideries. Detail of the Horses and Roses quilt.

Beads and Baubles

Sewing beads through all layers quilted the layers of the silk jacket.

Beads added to outline stitch highlight a feather motif on the Victorian quilt.

Beading

Great quantities of glass beads appear in Victorian needle arts. They were used in needlepoint, crochet, knitting, sewed onto cross stitch pieces and into elaborate patterns on velveteen.

Wonderful highlights on crazy quilts, beads can be sewn into patterns, used as flower centers, or just sewn on randomly. Add them to embroidery along patches in place of French knots. Use them to tack ribbons and lace motifs onto patches.

Glass seed beads are available in a range of sizes and in a variety of finishes such as transparent, opaque, silver lined, and metallic. Washability varies, so test-wash if using on a washable project.

Add beads last after all embroidery is finished, otherwise threads may catch on them. Also keep in mind that glass beads will add weight to a project.

Beads can be sewn on one at a time or several at once. You can also string a length of them and then couch them down.

A supported embroidery hoop can speed the process by allowing the free use of both hands.

Beaded needlepoint takes the form of pansies, nestled into leaves of silk ribbon embroidery on the Victorian quilt.

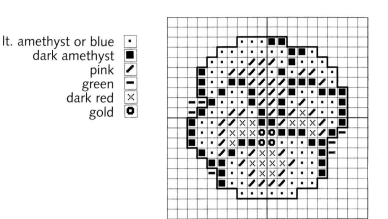

lt. amethyst or blue ·
dark amethyst ■
pink ╱
green ▬
dark red ✕
gold ◘

Beaded Needlepoint

Beaded needlepoint was a popular Victorian needle art. Worked in glass seed beads in small designs, this technique can make charming, small patch embellishments. Larger pieces however, can add too much weight to a quilt.

Work beaded pieces on a "soft" canvas such as cotton interlock. There are three ways that beads can be used in a counted design: working the entire design in beads, using beads for all except the background, and using them only for some highlights.

Use graphed designs intended for cross stitch or needlepoint, or create your own.

Match the size of the bead to the canvas. For instance, size 11 beads fit a 16-count canvas. Sew on the beads using a half cross stitch so that all the beads slant in the same direction.

Charms

Charms can be added to silk ribbon and other embroideries on crazy quilts. They make attractive accents on wall quilts and other small projects, but it is not advisable to use them on quilts and clothing where they can catch on threads.

Buttons

Buttons of all types and sizes can be sewn onto crazy quilts, especially wall quilts and other small projects. Sew them on in clusters, overlapping them slightly. Use doll-size pearl buttons for small, delicate touches, flower and bow centers, and to tack down lace motifs and other trims.

Look for interesting buttons made of wood, bone, leather, shells, glass, metal, porcelain, and other materials. Antique buttons can also be found, as well as reproductions of antiques.

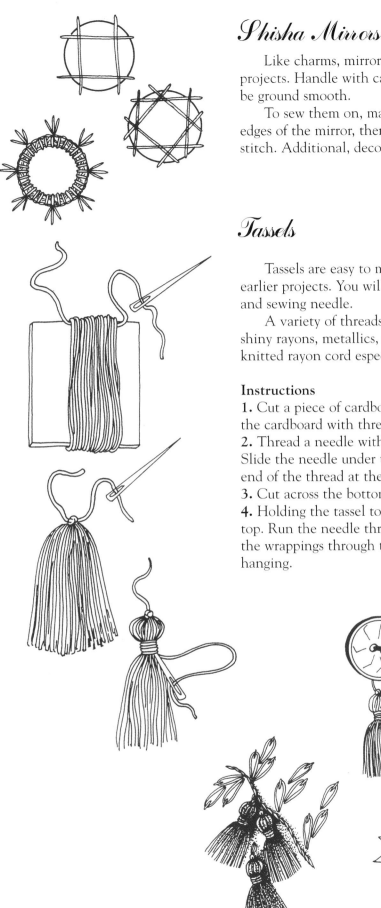

Shisha Mirrors

Like charms, mirrors are best placed on wall hangings and smaller projects. Handle with care; they are made of glass and the edges may not be ground smooth.

To sew them on, make a series of straight stitches overlapping the edges of the mirror, then cover the stitches with overlapping buttonhole stitch. Additional, decorative stitches may be added around the mirrors.

Tassels

Tassels are easy to make and a great way to use up extra threads from earlier projects. You will need threads, a small piece of cardboard, scissors, and sewing needle.

A variety of threads and thread types can be combined. Try mixing shiny rayons, metallics, and matte cottons in a tassel. Or, use Bunka, a knitted rayon cord especially for tassel-making.

Instructions

1. Cut a piece of cardboard to the length of tassel you are making. Wrap the cardboard with thread until it is as thick as you want it to be.
2. Thread a needle with about one yard of the same or matching thread. Slide the needle under the wrappings, and tie a knot about 6" from the end of the thread at the top of the tassel.
3. Cut across the bottom to remove it from the cardboard.
4. Holding the tassel together, wrap the long end of the thread near the top. Run the needle through the tassel several times to secure, then under the wrappings through to the top. Tie the ends at the top. Make a loop for hanging.

Fabrications

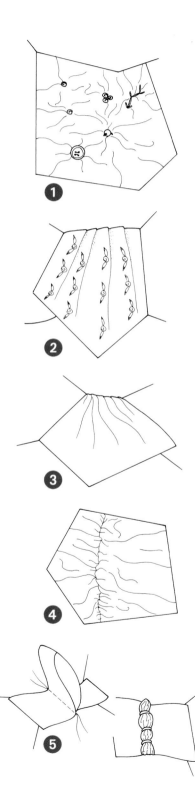

A scrunched patch is held in place by embroidery on the Victorian quilt.

Texturing Fabrics

A fun and easy way to add dimensionality to a quilt top is to add folds, gathers, and scrunches to a patch as it is laid onto the foundation. Silk fabrics are especially wonderful for these techniques.

Begin with a piece of patch fabric that is too large for the space. "Remove" the excess by folding, tucking, pleating, gathering, or scrunching. Hold the scrunches and folds in place with embroidery stitches or buttons.

1. Scrunch and tack the excess fabric, creating "puffs" between tacks. To tack, use French Knots, beads, buttons, or short lines of Feather stitching.

2. Arrange the free end into folds or pleats, pin and baste them in place. Later, as you embroider the quilt, silk ribbon or other embroidery can be worked on the folds to tack them in place.

3. Run a gathering thread along the free end, pull up until the end fits the space, and end off.

4. Run a gathering thread across the patch, pull up to gather, and fasten off.

5. Leaving two opposite sides of the patch free, run a basting thread as shown. Couch the excess fabric with embroidery ribbon or thread. Finish the patch by hemming the free end, or place the adjoining patch over it. Pin, then baste.

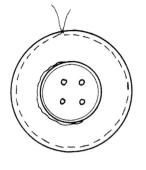

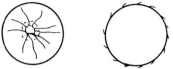

Fabric Overlays

Place a sheer or lace fabric over an opaque one to use as a patch. Use netting, tulle, gauzes, organza, and other sheer fabrics and laces. These are useful in landscape pieces to create the effects of fog, water, and mist.

Covering Buttons

These are not the same as the covered buttons used for clothing! They are a great way to use leftover pieces of your hand-dyed silks, and are sewn flat onto a patch with no shank. Covered buttons are attractive placed at the corners of patches, on fans, and as flower centers. Attach tassels to them if you like. You will need some plain plastic 2- or 4-hole buttons, small pieces of fabric, cotton batting, and sewing thread.

Instructions

1. Cut a piece of fabric twice as large as the button. Cut a piece of batting the same size as the button. Run a basting thread around the outer edge of the fabric.
2. Place the batting inside the fabric and the button on top of it, and pull up the gathers. Fasten with a few small stitches, then slipstitch the button to a patch.

Covered buttons and silk tassels await placement on the Ladies and Fans quilt.

Organza Sandwich

Save all of your silk trimmings, tiny fabric scraps, and thread and ribbon ends to make original patches. The example was sewn by machine, but you may also consider using embroidery or other handstitching to hold the layers in place.

An Organza Sandwich patch on the Victorian quilt.

Instructions

1. Cut the organza into two patch-size pieces each the same. Place the silk trimmings between them (like a sandwich); pin.
2. Work stitching over the entire piece. Make the stitching close enough so it adequately holds the trimmings in place.

Monogramming

Used to decorate household linens, monogramming is one of the needle arts practiced by Victorian stitchers. Monograms are appropriate patch decorations on crazy quilts.

A variety of stitches may be used, the most common being Satin, Backstitch, and Outline stitch. Floral embroideries may be added. Use one or more strands of cotton, rayon, or silk floss.

Instructions

1. Choose an alphabet style, two are given here. If you will be overlapping two or more letters onto each other, consider making them two different sizes. Redraw the letters in the desired sizes onto tracing paper. Cut them out and arrange as desired, then retrace the monogram.

2. Transfer letters to fabric using the Tracing Paper Transfer Method, see page 32.

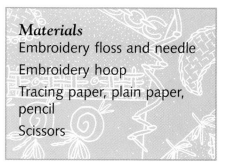

Materials
Embroidery floss and needle
Embroidery hoop
Tracing paper, plain paper, pencil
Scissors

A monogram and a tea rose were combined in this shadowbox detail.

The letter "C" was appliquéd, then embroidered in this Canadian crazy quilt detail. Collection of Rocky Mountain Quilts, York Village, Maine.

Suggestions for Embroidery

Outline the letter in outline stitch, and fill in solid areas with satin or padded satin stitch. Victorian instructions call for making the padded stitches thicker at the center and thinner at the outer edges. Making more of the filler stitches toward the center, and fewer at the outer edges does this.

Outline a solid letter in backstitch and work satin stitch to fill in the letter. The satin stitch should cover the backstitching.

Outline the letter in outline stitch and fill in the solid areas with French knots.

Outline the letter with backstitch or outline stitch, and then work detached buttonhole stitch over them. Fill in the solid areas with French knots or satin stitch.

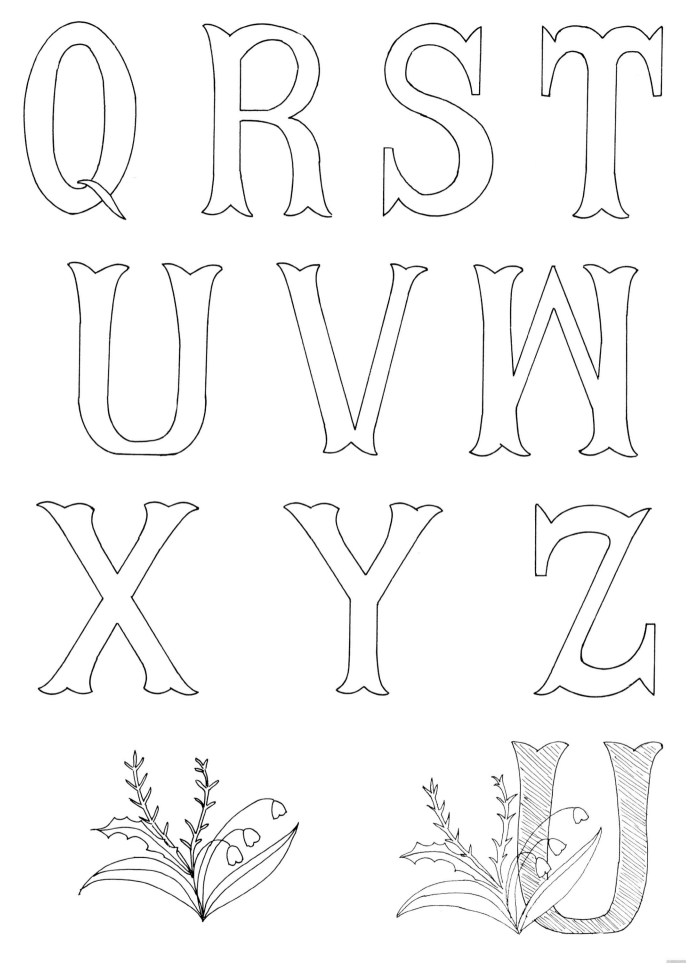

Punchneedle Embroidery

Punchneedle embroidery creates a rug-like pile on the surface of the fabric. Use it to form solid mats of sheared or looped pile, or to add random looping to other embroidery. Work it on individual pieces of fabric, or on a patched quilt top.

Punchneedle is worked on the wrong side of the fabric using a special hollow needle. As the needle is punched through the fabric and withdrawn, a loop is formed on the right side.

Punchneedles are available in several sizes for different fibers to be used, from crewel yarn to a single strand of silk floss. Follow the instructions that came with your needles, and experiment with different fibers. Wool, silk, and cotton threads often work best. The thread must slide through the eye of the needle easily, but yet not be too loose.

It is best worked on a patched quilt top, since the two layers of fabric better secure the loops than if only one fabric is used. The weave of the background fabric holds the loops in place.

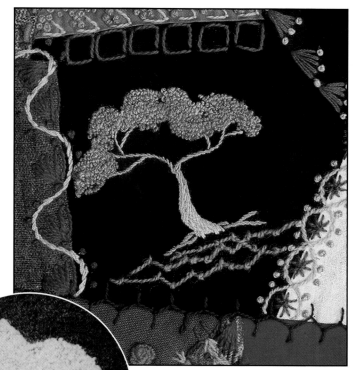

A fruit tree in full bloom is worked in outline stitch and punchneedle embroidery on the Horses and Roses quilt.

Soft and fuzzy creatures are likely subjects for punchneedle embroidery. Detail of the Horses and Roses quilt.

Instructions:

1. Draw or transfer a design onto the wrong side of the fabric. OR: begin with a design that was previously worked in outline stitch on the right side of the fabric (you will be punching on the wrong side).

2. Wrong side up, snugly fit the fabric into an embroidery hoop.

3. To thread the punchneedle, use the threader to bring the thread down through the shaft, then thread the eye from the concave side outward.

4. Begin to punch, keeping the tip of the needle in contact with the fabric between punches. Use a punch-slide rhythm as you work. Hold the needle vertically, or at a bit of a slant and with the opening facing upwards, or away from yourself. Trim thread ends close to the surface of the piece.

Tips:

Watch that the thread is unhindered and moving freely through the needle.

When filling in solid areas, work from side to side: left to right, then right to left, moving away from yourself.

To ensure a neat edge, work outline or backstitch around a design before punching.

Areas can be punched a second time to fill them in more, or to add a second shade or fiber.

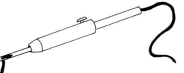

Materials
Set of punchneedles and a threader
Embroidery threads
Transferred design
Embroidery hoop
Scissors

Ribbonwork

Materials
Various types of fabric ribbons

Sewing thread and needle

Pins

Scissors

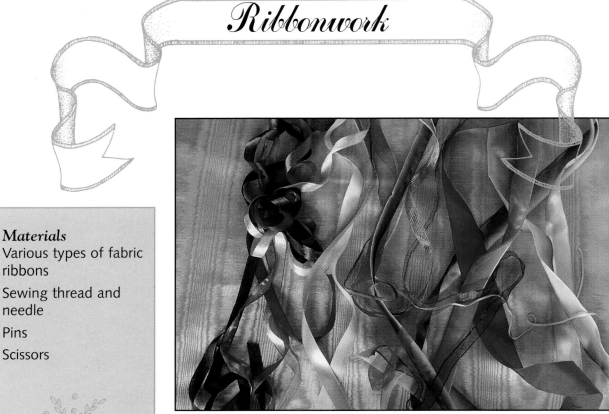

Wired and soft rayon, silk satin, nylon organdy, and other fabric ribbons for ribbon work.

For some real dimensionality, add some ribbonworked florals to your quilt top or project. Flowers crafted of wide, luxurious ribbons always seem to make a dramatic and bold statement.

First add a singular flower with a leaf, expanding into larger arrangements such as bouquets and sprays that spread out over a patch or more. Also use ribbons to make scrunched and gathered trims along the edges of patches, taking the place of embroidery.

Collect a variety of fabric ribbons in a range of widths, the kind that are made for sewing and needle arts. Some ribbons are wired along their edges, and these wires can be left in for shaping, or removed if not needed (simply slide them out).

Experiment with different ribbons to make the trims and flowers on these pages. Although some are better suited to wide or narrow ribbons, most of the flowers and trims can be made of many widths.

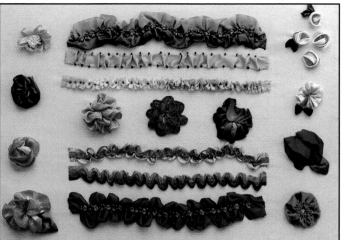

Ribbonworked flowers and trims.

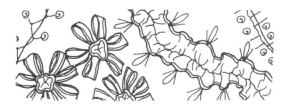

Making Bias Ribbons

You can make your own ribbons by cutting silk fabric on the bias; for this, lightweight silk fabrics are the best choice. (See Cutting Bias Strips, page 129.) Use them as they are, leaving the edges raw, or sew them into tubes and then press flat. Ruche and fold them into flowers the same as for ribbons.

Gathered and Couched Trims

Couch a ribbon directly onto a patch. Meander it as desired, and fasten its ends under patch edges. If you make the ribbon longer than needed, it can be scrunched as it couched. If needed, pin the scrunches in place before couching. Couch the trims with embroidery stitches, or beads, buttons, or silk ribbon embroidery. Or, gather the ribbon before couching it down.

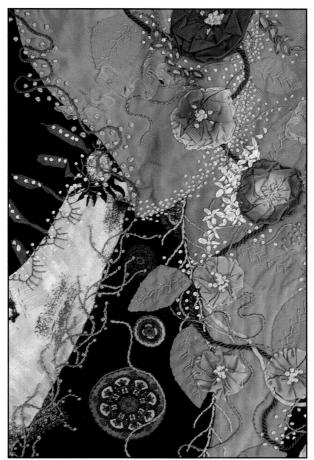

Couched ribbons on the Piano Shawl.

Run a thread along the center of the ribbon and then gather the ribbon.

Gather one or both edges of the ribbon.

Sew the gathering stitches in a zigzag fashion.

Velvet ribbons can be shaped and stuffed as demonstrated by this antique velvet pillow. Collection of Rocky Mountain Quilts, York Village, Maine.

Gathered Flowers

Choose a length of ribbon according to how full you want the flower. A lightly-gathered flower will look different than a very full one made with a longer piece of ribbon. Experiment with various lengths.

Circle flower. Sew the long ends of a length of ribbon together then run a gathering thread along one edge. Pull up tightly, and fasten off. Shape the flower while tacking it onto a crazy patch. For a variation, use two ribbons of different widths and/or colors held together as one.

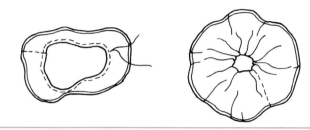

Winding flower. Edge-gather or ruche a length of ribbon. Sew one end of the ribbon to a crazy patch then wind the remainder of it around while stitching it down.

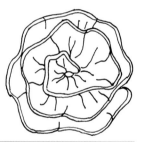

Double flower. Follow instructions for the circle or winding flower, but gather the ribbon along its center. Stitch the gathered line to a crazy patch, folding the two edges upward to form a double row of petals.

Berries and buds. Sew a short length of ribbon into a circle and then gather both long edges. Tack them down and use them for buds, berries, and some flower types. A pinch of stuffing can be added inside the berry or flower.

Folded Flowers and Leaf

Accordion Rose.

1. Thread a needle with matching thread and set it aside. Begin at the center of a length of ribbon, using about 9" of ⅜", or 12" of ¾" wide ribbon. Fold the left end of the ribbon down. Fold the same end upwards and to the back. Fold the right end backwards. Continue to fold, alternating ends and always folding backwards.
2. Hold the final fold firmly, let go of the previous folds, and slowly pull one end downward. Stop pulling as soon as the rose forms.
3. Secure by stitching through the base, then the center of the flower. Trim the ends of the ribbon off, and stitch the rose to a crazy patch.

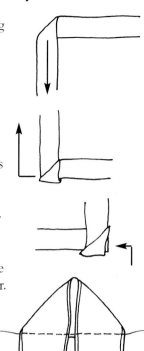

Prairie point leaf. The finished size of the leaf depends on the ribbon's width. Fold the ribbon and run a gathering thread as shown. Pull up to gather, fasten off, and trim the ends. Stitch the leaf to a crazy patch, placing a flower over the gathered end.

Tea rose or rosebud.

1. To make a large rosebud, use about 14" of 1½" wide ribbon. Thread a needle with matching thread and set aside. Remove the wire from the lower edge of the ribbon if it is wired. Fold one end downward and then wrap the long end of the ribbon loosely around the fold, finishing by folding the end downward. Sew through the base several times, then wrap the thread around several times and fasten off.
2. Trim the ribbon ends close to the stitching.
3. Fold the lowest petal downward to conceal the stitching, and sew the rosebud to a patch. Arrange the petals and tack them in place with a few stitches.

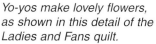
Yo-yos make lovely flowers, as shown in this detail of the Ladies and Fans quilt.

Ribbon Flowers and Yo-yos

Winding rose. Use a long needle and make this directly on a crazy patch. Secure one end of the ribbon by putting the needle through it. Wind the ribbon around the needle until the flower is as full as you want it. Tuck in the end of the ribbon, thread a second needle, and stitch the "petals" in place.

Looped ribbon flowers. Use ¼" satin, or 4mm or 7mm silk ribbon. Make them in hand, or directly on a patch. Holding the center of the flower, fold the ribbon into loops. Securely sew the loops at the center. Add a small gathered flower to the center to conceal the stitching.

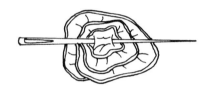

Yo-yos. Made of fabric, not ribbon, these also make wonderful flowers. Cut a circle of fabric, 4" or the size desired—silk jacquards are a good choice! Fold the outer edge under about ¼" and baste close to this edge. Pull up to gather, and fasten off. Slipstitch the yo-yo to a patch. Arrange yo-yos in side, or ¾ views as well as full-face. Add some French knots inside the opening.

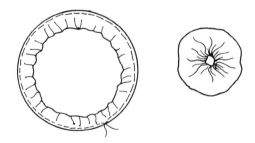

Bias Ribbon Flowers

Ribbon flower petals. Make 4 to 12 petals, depending on the desired full-ness of the finished flower. Using wide ribbon or bias scraps of fabric, cut two 2" x 3" pieces.

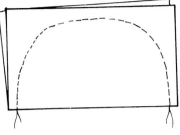

Place the two pieces right sides together and sew as shown. Trim the seam; turn and press the petal. Repeat for the remaining petals.

For each petal, baste along the base; gather and then fasten off. Sew the petals to each other, adding one at a time. Sew the flower to a patch adding a leaf or two. Then take sev-eral stitches down through the center of the flower to secure it in place on a crazy patch.

Bias ribbon rolled rose. Thread a needle with matching thread and set aside.

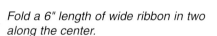

Fold a 6" length of wide ribbon in two along the center.

Roll the folded ribbon two or three times around the tip of your index fin-ger, folding both ends downward to conceal the raw edges.

Slide the rose off your finger, holding it firmly. Stitch through the base, then wrap the thread around several times and fasten off. Trim ribbon close to the thread. Open out the rose and slipstitch the outer petals to a patch. Then make several stitches down through the center to secure it in place.

Silk Ribbon Embroidery

If you haven't yet tried silk ribbon embroidery, put it on your "to do" list. It was one of the many needle arts practiced by Victorian ladies, and makes an ideal embellishment for crazy quilting. It's also very easy to learn and to do.

Use the basic embroidery stitches in addition to the ribbon stitches here, but with silk ribbons in place of threads or floss. Although it can be worked on separate scraps of fabric, it is easiest to do on a patched crazy quilt top or project, so the ends of ribbons can be fastened into the foundation.

The most common subject matter is florals; the stitches dimensionally portray the flower parts. A ribbon stitch makes a leaf or petal, a French knot a flower center, a lazy daisy stitch a bud, and so on.

Silk has a weightless, airy quality, imparting a painterly characteristic to this needle art, a trait that is enhanced if hand-dyed ribbons are used.

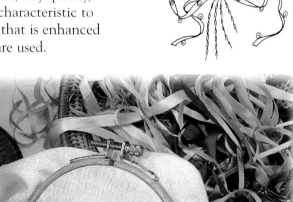

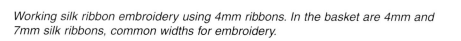

Working silk ribbon embroidery using 4mm ribbons. In the basket are 4mm and 7mm silk ribbons, common widths for embroidery.

Materials
Size 18 chenille needle
4" embroidery hoop
Silk ribbons
Scissors

Variegated silk ribbons can be purchased, or you can easily dye them yourself. Dyeing instructions are on pages 102.

Silk embroidery ribbons come in widths of 2mm, 4mm, 7mm, and wider. The 4mm width is the most commonly used.

Other types of ribbons can be used, but they will not embroider in the same way, although you might like to try them for adding special effects.

Threading the Needle

Place one end of the ribbon through the eye of the needle, then run the needle through the ribbon, about ¼" to ½" from the same end. Pull on the long end to settle the "knot" into the eye of the needle.

To fasten on, make a tiny stitch on the back of the fabric, then run the needle up through the tail of the stitch.

Tips

Use short lengths of ribbon, about 12" to 14". Longer ribbons may begin to wear and fray at the edges.

Use a size 18 chenille needle when stitching with 4mm and 7mm ribbons, making a hole in the fabric that is large enough for the ribbon to slide through easily, reducing wear.

A small, 3" or 4" embroidery hoop will keep the fabric smooth and yet allow your fingers to reach the stitches.

Choose high quality embroidery ribbons.

Make the stitches loosely, observing each as it forms, and stopping before the ribbon is pulled too tightly.

Allow the ribbon to untwist between stitches.

Vary a stitch by twisting the ribbon before making the stitch. Try this with straight, fly, feather, and other stitches.

Ironing the ribbons before using can give a little extra body to them.

To press the finished embroidery, place it face down on a towel-covered ironing board, and press lightly with a dry iron. Take care to not flatten the embroidery.

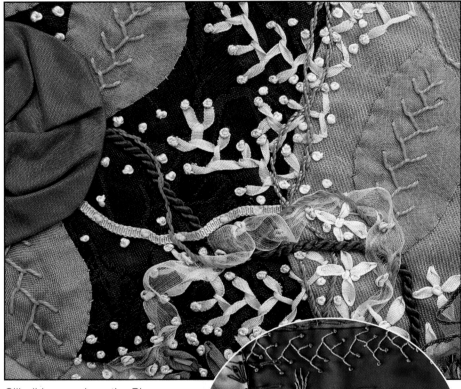

Silk ribbon work on the Piano Shawl.

Silk ribbon used in combination with size 12 pearl cotton to fashion a duo of moss roses on the Victorian quilt.

This vintage corner block detail shows silk ribbon embroidered daisy petals. Collection of Rocky Mountain Quilts, York Village, Maine.

Silk Ribbon Stitches

The following stitches are unique to silk ribbon embroidery. In addition to these, many other stitches are excellent for silk ribbon work, including:

Straight stitch	Chain stitch rose	Fern stitch
Outline stitch	Fly stitch	French knot
Outline stitch rose	Feather stitch	Pistil stitch
Lazy daisy stitch	Double feather stitch	Woven stitches

Ribbon Stitch

Smooth the ribbon onto the surface of the fabric, then pierce the end of the stitch and pull through. A variation is to allow the ribbon to "pouf," making a slightly rounded stitch. These are excellent for leaves and flower petals. Make them in clusters for treetops.

Pierced Loop Stitch

Make this stitch the same as the ribbon stitch, but sink the needle near to where it first came through the fabric. Keeping the ribbon smooth, pull through, stopping when the loop is the size desired. In a motif, work these last so other stitches won't pull them loose. Use these for flower petals and centers, and for filler stitches in embroideries.

Woven Rose

Make five spokes using ribbon or thread. Then, attach a second ribbon and, starting from the center, weave around until the spokes are filled.

Couching

Thread two needles with matching or contrasting ribbons. Fasten on the first ribbon and arrange it, pinning in place. Fasten on the second ribbon and make French knots or small stitches to hold the first one in place. Couched streamers and bows are elegant additions to floral embroideries.

Detail of a cottage garden scene worked in soft shades of hand-dyed silk ribbons on dark-green linen fabric.

Creating a Rose Motif

1. Begin with several woven roses to establish the placement of the design. Motifs can be placed to fit into spaces such as corners and borders in addition to patch centers. Add leaves of lazy daisy or ribbon stitches.

2. Add feather or fern stitches to begin filling in the background. Add several rosebuds, making each out of a lazy daisy with a fly stitch.

3. Add twisted straight stitch flowers, and finish by scattering French knots throughout.

Crazy quilt detail. Collection of The Brick Store museum, Kennebunk, Maine.

Wool Embroidery

Wool embroidery is worked on patches and along seams on the Horses and Roses quilt.

Wool embroidery shares many of the characteristics of silk ribbon work. It is dimensional, easy to learn and do, and adaptable to many uses. And, like silk ribbon work, the stitches form flower parts and leaves. Scatter wool embroideries along patch seams, or create bouquets within patches.

Use wool threads that are made for embroidery such as tapestry or Persian. These include Broder Medici, Paternayan Persian, and Impressions (50 percent silk/50 percent wool). Collect these and any other wool threads you can find; they can be mixed and matched. The best background fabric is wool, although other fabrics can also be used. Try the stitches given here, and experiment with others as well. See Victorian Stitches, pages 34 to 73.

Materials
Wool threads

Chenille needles in sizes to go with the threads

Embroidery hoop if needed

Scissors

Bullion

Tips:

Use a chenille needle that is large enough to make a hole in the fabric for the wool thread to pass through easily.

When working through two layers of fabric, pull the thread all the way through to form each part of a stitch. This reduces wear on the thread.

Begin and end by making two or three tiny stitches on the back of the piece (no knots).

Bullion-stitch roses worked in wool on the Horses and Roses quilt.

Stitch Roses and Flowers

To form roses, work overlapping Bullion knots around a center of two shorter bullions, French knots, or padded satin stitch. Add various embroidery stitches to bullion knots to make other types of flowers.

Blanket Stitch Flowers

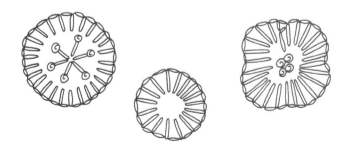

Make large, round flowers by working blanket stitch in a circular fashion. To make neat, even circles you may wish to first draw the outer circle of the flower onto the fabric using tailor's chalk.

Lazy Daisy Flowers

Lazy daisy stitches make pretty flowers and petals.

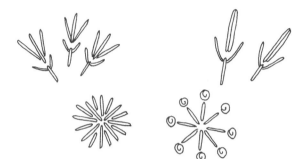

Straight Stitch Flowers

Groupings of straight stitches create different flower forms.

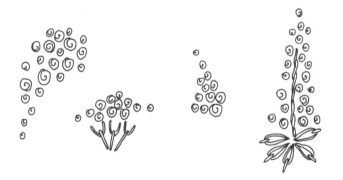

French Knot Flowers

Lilacs, wisteria, Queen Anne's lace, lupine, and other flowers can be represented by groupings of French knots. For natural-looking flowers, vary the sizes of stitches by the number of times the thread is wound around the needle, and by winding the thread loosely for some and tightly for others.

Star Stitch Flowers

Very small star stitch flowers appear as dots, and are useful for centers or small flowers.

Stitches for Leaves

Some of the stitches that can be used for leaves include fishbone, feather, straight, fern, and stacked lazy daisy.

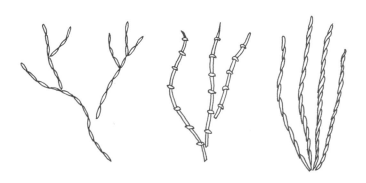

Stems and Branches

Use backstitch, couching, or outline stitch for stems and branches.

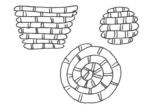

Weaving

Weave baskets, vases, and flower centers.

Detail of an 1898 wool crazy quilt. Collection of Rocky Mountain Quilts, York Village, Maine.

Paint, Dye, and Transfer Methods

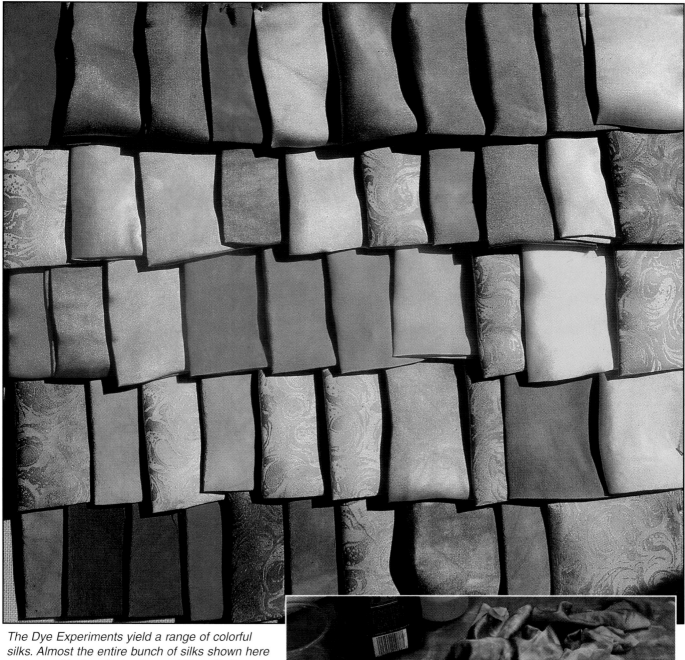

The Dye Experiments yield a range of colorful silks. Almost the entire bunch of silks shown here were used in the silk Ladies and Fans Quilt.

If you dye and paint your own fabrics, you will never be running around searching for the "right" color. Buy a yard or two each of several differently textured fabrics in white or off-white, and some dye and paint supplies and then get ready to have some fun.

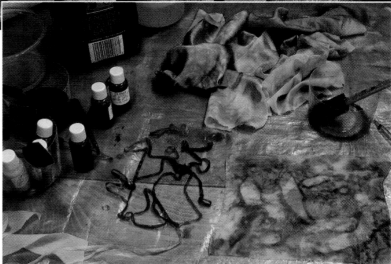

Using dye to create unusual patch fabrics and ribbons.

Dyeing Silks

Materials

Instant-setting silk dyes, ½ oz. bottle each of red, yellow, blue, and black

Distilled water

4 quarter-yard pieces of white or natural silk fabrics, each a different type of silk

Any desired silk ribbons, trims, threads

½ cup measure

3 small containers such as jars or plastic, do not re-use in the kitchen

8 or more eye droppers

Pair of tongs

Large piece of plastic to cover your work surface

Silks are the easiest fibers to dye; simply dye, rinse, dry, press, and use them. Collect natural-color or white silk fabrics in different textures: Habotai, dupioni, crepe, jacquard, satin, and so on. Also collect some satin silk ribbons and silk ribbons for embroidery, and any other undyed silk trims you can find. It is such a simple process that you can dye a few pieces at a time, and it is easy to achieve an almost infinite range of color shades. Do the dye experiments to learn how to mix dyes to get the colors you want.

There are different types of dyes for silks. One is instant-setting dye and needs no further treatment. Another requires a dye-setting additive after allowing the fabrics to set for 24 hours. Both are easy to use, and can be done in small amounts. The instructions here are for an instant-setting dye. If you use a different type, follow the instructions that came with the dye.

Instructions:

1. Cover your work surface with plastic (and wear rubber gloves if you will be sticking your fingers into the dye). Cut each fat quarter into 12 pieces. Pre-wash the fabrics, and keep them damp.

2. Use one eyedropper for each dye bottle, and one for each container of dye mixture to stir the fabrics. Follow the dye experiments to yield 10 fabric patches for each of the dye colors.

3. To dye evenly, stir the silks for several minutes while in the dye bath. For a mottled effect, crumple the silks into the dye, and leave them for a couple of minutes. Then, turn them over, and leave for a couple of minutes again.

4. Remove the fabrics from the dye using tongs. Allow them to drip, then set aside.

5. When all dyeing is finished, wash the fabrics with mild soap and rinse under running water. Roll them in a clean towel to remove excess moisture. Line dry, then press. Wash all containers and tools in soapy water.

Ideas to Try

Spread out some silk ribbons and trims on your work surface. While doing the dye experiments, randomly place drops of dye on them to make them multi-colored.

Working inside a cardboard box, draw a Popsicle stick across a dye-loaded toothbrush to splatter dye on pieces of silk.

Once you find a color you really like, continue to dye pieces of fabric, adding water each time to obtain a range of shades.

Try over-dyeing already dyed silks—either pieces you've done, or commercially dyed silks.

Sprinkle coarse salt onto a piece of fabric and then place drops of dye onto it. Allow the dye to set, then rinse thoroughly.

Dye Experiments

Do each of the dye experiments to yield 40 or more differently colored patches. The experiments are an exercise in mixing dye colors, and achieving pastels and browns. To create deeper shades of the browns, do the experiments, but skip the second column of the charts. To replicate specific colors, you may wish to keep notes on how much water and dye were used.

Some of the colors overlap.

For instance, green can be derived from both the yellow and blue experiments. In these cases, adjust the dyes to create different shades of green each time.

You may find that the black experiments yield the most interesting shades including teal, mauve, dusty green and purple. You may wish to experiment further to find additional shades. Keep in mind that the fabrics will dry considerably lighter than they are when wet.

Dye Experiment: YELLOW

Measure 1/2 cup of distilled water into a container, and add drops of yellow dye. Add and stir until the mixture is a medium yellow. Dye one piece of silk to check that this is a medium shade.

Divide the mixture into each of three containers.

Dye Experiment: BLUE

Measure 1/2 cup of distilled water into a container, and add drops of blue dye. Add and stir until the mixture is a medium blue. Dye one piece of silk to check that this is a medium shade.

Divide the mixture into each of three containers.

Dye Experiment: RED

Measure 1/2 cup of distilled water into a container, and add drops of red dye. Add and stir until the mixture is a medium red. Dye one piece of silk to check that this is a medium shade.

Divide the mixture into each of three containers.

Dye Experiment: BLACK

Measure 1/2 cup of distilled water into a container, and add drops of black dye. Add and stir until the mixture is a medium gray. Dye one piece of silk to check that this is a medium shade.

Divide the mixture into each of three containers.

	Column 1	Column 2	Column 3
	To create mixed colors, add several drops of the following, and dye a piece of silk in each:	Then add the following to obtain a lighter shade of the color in column 1, and dye another piece of silk in each:	Then add a drop or two of the following to obtain browned shades, and dye another piece of silk in each:
Container 1	Red (= orange)	water	Blue
Container 2	Blue (= green)	water	Black & Red
Container 3	Black (= chartreuse)	water	Black
Container 1	Red (= royal purple)	water	Black & Yellow
Container 2	Yellow (= green)	water	Red (= lt. moss green)
Container 3	Black (= deep blue)	water	Black
Container 1	Yellow (= orange)	water	Blue
Container 2	Blue (= purple)	water	Black
Container 3	Black	water	Black
Container 1	Red	water	Blue
Container 2	Blue, Yellow and 1 or 2 drops of Red	water	Black
Container 3	Yellow and 1 drop of Red	water	Red

Painting on Fabric

Victorian ladies did paintings on silk or velvet, and sometimes included them in their crazy quilts. They used oil paints. The acrylics we have now are easier and less messy. They are water-based so they can be thinned and cleaned up with water; although, by heat setting, they become permanent on fabric.

Unless you already have painting skills, you can learn how to paint flowers and simple objects by following instructions in a book or taking a class. There are many books available; choose one (or more) that portrays a style you'd like to try. Once you get started, subject matter will make itself apparent; look around you for ideas of things to paint.

It isn't necessary to paint pictures and scenes. You can also apply paint in ways that create interesting effects, such as splattering, dripping, washes, and watercolor effects. These often make interesting backgrounds for embroidery and embellishment.

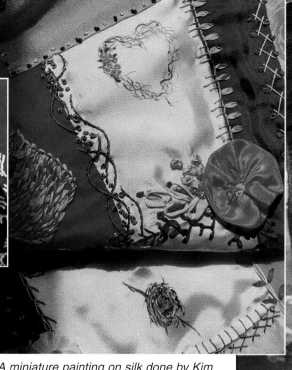

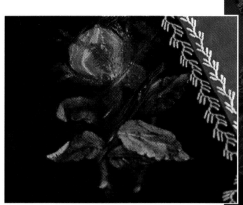

On a mid-1800s crazy quilt, a rose was painted on black velvet. Detail. The Brick Store Museum, Kennebunk, Maine.

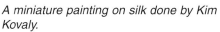

A miniature painting on silk done by Kim Kovaly.

An elaborate painting on velvet makes a beautiful sashing on this mid-1800s crazy quilt. Detail. The Brick Store Museum, Kennebunk, Maine.

Materials
- Acrylic paints in tubes or jars: red, blue, yellow, black, and white
- Artist's brushes in a variety of sizes
- Bowls or small pots for mixing
- Water
- Palette or plate for mixing colors
- Masking tape and cardboard or embroidery hoop

There are two basic techniques for painting: wet brush, and dry brush. For dry brush, slightly dampen the brush, dip it into the paint, and brush it onto the fabric. Fine lines and details can be done this way. For wet brush, dip the brush in water and leave it wet. Use paint thinned with water. As the paint is brushed onto the fabric, it will spread out. Different effects can be obtained by having the fabric damp, or very wet.

See Color Theory on page 14 for achieving a range of colors by mixing the primary and secondary colors. Almost any type of fabric can be used—experiment to find those that work best for you.

Instructions:

1. Pre-wash the fabric, allow it to dry, and press. Place the fabric into an embroidery hoop, or tape it onto cardboard.

2. Do the paintings following the method and style of your choice.

3. Set the finished paintings aside for 24 hours to dry completely. Heat set.

> **Acrylic paints must be heat-set to make them permanent. Place a press cloth over the painted area. Heat the iron to the correct temperature setting for the fabric, and hold the iron on for 30 seconds. Repeat to cover the entire painted area.**

Ideas to Try

Achieve different effects by either stroking or dabbing with the brush.

Create rainbow effects by placing two or more colors on the brush at a time.

Use your fingers, foam brushes, sponges, crumpled paper, or other implements to apply the paint.

Using a toothbrush inside a cardboard box, splatter the paint onto the fabric.

Drip the paint onto the fabric.

Marbling

Marbling is wonderful fun and you will love the results. A kit from Dharma Trading (see Sources) includes the basic supplies you will need. This kit includes alum, carrageenan, a dispersing agent that is added to the paints, and three colors of paint.

I used an 8" square aluminum baking pan which nicely holds a quart of carrageenan, making my fabric pieces about 6" square. Use any size pan that you want, but the pan must be slightly larger than the fabric. Mix up enough carrageenan to fill the pan a little more than an inch.

Carrageenan mixed with water creates a gelatinous solution that enables paints to stay on top of it. When the fabric treated with alum is laid onto the painted surface it absorbs the paint.

All set up for marbling. You need paints, pans, eyedroppers, and swirling tools.

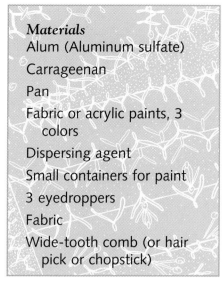

Materials

Alum (Aluminum sulfate)

Carrageenan

Pan

Fabric or acrylic paints, 3 colors

Dispersing agent

Small containers for paint

3 eyedroppers

Fabric

Wide-tooth comb (or hair pick or chopstick)

Instructions:

1. Prepare the carrageenan a day ahead. I used 1 tablespoon dissolved in a quart of hot water. Do this in a quart jar, and shake and stir like crazy until the carrageenan dissolves. Or, use a blender, blending for about a minute. Place the jar of carrageenan in the refrigerator for 24 hours. The next day, take it out of the refrigerator and pour it into the pan. Let it warm to room temperature.

2. Prepare the fabric by pre-washing and drying. Dissolve the alum, using ⅛ cup of alum in a quart of hot water. Let it cool to room temperature.

3. Dip the fabric into the alum, and take it out immediately. Hang up the fabric to drip dry, or lay it out to dry flat. Cut the fabric into pieces slightly smaller than the pan.

4. Prepare to marble. Place one paint color into each of the small containers. Add small amounts of water and stir until they are the consistency of whole milk. Use the eyedroppers to stir. Add a drop of dispersing agent and to each color.

5. Using an eyedropper, carefully place drops of paint onto the surface of the carrageenan. The paint should spread out a little bit. Keep adding paint, using drops of all three colors until the surface is covered.

6. Take the comb or chopstick and pull it through the paint. Make swirls, straight lines … experiment! When the surface is as you like it, carefully place a piece of

fabric on top. Leave it there for about five seconds and then lift it off carefully.

7. Rinse the fabric under cool, running water and lay flat or hang to dry. Dry completely, then heat set according to instructions for the paint.

8. To continue, add more drops of paint to the carrageenan and swirl again. Or, remove the paint with strips of newspaper and start all over again. I sometimes like to simply swirl and then add a piece of fabric to obtain pastel shades.

9. Save the carrageenan in the refrigerator to reuse it within a few days.

Troubleshooting: If at first you don't succeed, don't give up! The hardness of the water can make a difference: try using distilled water. You may need to adjust the amount of carrageenan-to-water mixture, using more or less. It should be thick enough that the paints float on top. If a little paint goes to the bottom, that's okay. You can also try thinning the paints a little more.

Only three paint colors were used to create this assortment of marbled silk fabrics.

Stamping

Stamping is a simple matter of placing objects into paint and stamping them onto fabric. Experiment on scrap fabrics before using your good fabrics.

Leaves make excellent "stamps" for fabric decoration.

Materials
Acrylic paints, water, brush
  or something to stir with
Palette or plate
Objects for stamping
Newspaper
Fabric

Instructions

1. On the palette, mix the acrylic paint with water until it is well thinned and spread out.
2. Dab the object into the paint a few times, then place it onto the fabric. Cover it with newspaper, and press down for a second or two. If the print comes out too heavy with paint for details to show, water the paint down a little more, spread it more thinly, or dab the object more gently.

Foiling

Foiling does not use paint, but is included here because it is another way to do stamping. Foiling shows up well because of the shine of the foil, and it sometimes produces a raised effect on the surface of the fabric.

Look around for objects that will stamp well, and practice on scrap fabrics before using your good fabrics.

Instructions:

1. Fold the towel and place it onto your work surface to make a padded surface. Place the fabric onto the towel.
2. Use the brush or foam applicator to apply adhesive to the stamping object. Stamp the object onto the fabric. Do this carefully so it stamps neatly. Depending on the object, you may need to use a tweezers to lift it off the fabric. Repeat for each stamped image. Set the stamped fabric aside to dry. Allow it to dry completely; this can take up to three or four hours.
3. Place the stamped fabric on the ironing board and heat the iron to the cotton setting. Place a sheet of the foil right side up onto the fabric. Experiment to find out how much pressure to apply to the iron. I found that sometimes I needed a lot of pressure, and other times almost none. Peel off the foil immediately after ironing. If areas didn't "take," the foil can be re-used until all of the color is removed from it.
The finished piece can be gently washed, but do not put it into a dryer. This will remove the foil. Use a press cloth when pressing.

Materials
Special adhesive and foil
  (see Sources)
Objects for stamping
Brush or foam applicator
An old towel
Fabric
Dry iron, ironing board

Foiling is a fun way to add design to a fabric's surface.

Stenciling

Materials

Cotton velveteen fabric, pre-washed and dried

Freezer paper, pencil

Craft knife and smooth cardboard

Smooth corrugated cardboard larger than the design

Stencil brush, ¾" or 1"

Acrylic paints in your choice of colors

Palette or plate

Sewing pins

Water

Stenciling paint onto velveteen fabric produces a clean-edge design with an almost luminescent effect from the paint. Freezer paper works well for making a stencil that is used one or two times. To use a stencil more than twice, cut it from a sturdier material. Use low-napped 100 percent cotton velveteen fabric.

Instructions:

1. Lay a piece of freezer paper over the design, and trace its outlines. Place this on the smooth cardboard, and cut along the lines using the craft knife.

2. Place the velveteen onto the corrugated cardboard, then the stencil with the plastic side down.

Pin into the cardboard to hold everything in place.

3. Mix the color or colors that will be used. You can leave the paints partly unmixed to get a varied effect to the painting. If the velveteen is dark, add plenty of white to the color so it shows up well. Do not add much water to the paint. If it is too wet, the color will be pulled under the stencil.

4. Dab the brush in the paint, then on the palette to remove excess. Holding the brush vertically, stencil the design by tapping the brush repeatedly until sufficient color is transferred. Remove the stencil and allow the paint to dry.

5. Heat set. Embroider the details.

A detail from the Shadow box.

Tools and materials for stenciling on fabric.

Photo Transfer

A photographic image on fabric is not a new idea. Crazy quilts of the late 1800s often include an image or two that is a photo on silk. All it takes is a special transfer paper, and the use of a color laser copier at a copy shop. The same can be done by computer, using an inkjet printer.

Materials
Photo transfer paper
Use of a color laser
   photocopier
OR
Computer, software, inkjet
   printer
Images: photos or antique
   postcards
Fabric scraps, iron

Instructions:

1. Choose several images, photos you have taken, or antique post-cards, for instance. Have them copied onto the transfer paper, or do this by computer. Should you need help in getting the computer to do what you want it to, there are online resources, or consult Jean Ray Laury's book, *The Photo Transfer Handbook, Snap It, Print It, Stitch It!* Include, also, several smaller images so you can test the transfer on your fabric.
2. Cut the images apart so they can be used separately. Select one of the small, test images. Position it carefully on the fabric, checking that the fabric lies smoothly. Press, using the iron setting that is indicated for your transfer paper. If the fabric scorches, place a sheet of plain paper between fabric and iron. If the test comes out OK, proceed with the remaining transfers.
3. Use the images as patches, or cut them out and appliqué them onto quilt patches. Add silk ribbon and other embroidery around them.

Photos of roses from my garden, and antique postcards are waiting to be photocopied onto transfer paper. A rose photo transferred onto the Ladies and Fans quilt has silk ribbon embroidered leaves added to it.

Rubbings

This technique involves taking rubbings from objects with interesting surfaces; in this case, antique butterstamps that were once used to imprint patterns into butter. Do not use plain crayons or pastels for this. For permanence on fabric, they must have dye in them. Follow any instructions that came with them.

A butterstamp wrapped in plastic for doing rubbings on silk fabrics.

Materials

Fabric crayons or pastels

Objects with 3-D surfaces: wooden buttermolds, gravestones, leaves, lace, etc.

Lightweight plastic if needed to protect the object

Tape, elastics, etc.

Iron

Several sheets of plain paper

Patches on the Butterstamp Quilt are rubbings taken from antique butterstamps.

Instructions

1. If using wooden butterstamps, first cover them in thin plastic to avoid dyeing the wood.

2. Place a piece of silk fabric over the object and either hold it in place tightly, or fasten it on with tape or elastics. Lightly rub the crayon over the object until the design shows up.

3. Remove the fabric from the print. Iron the fabric between two sheets of clean, white paper on an ironing board that is adequately protected with paper or scrap fabric. This sets the dye and removes the grease from the crayon. Repeat, using clean paper, to be sure the grease is removed.

4. Wash each rubbing separately. Line dry, and press.

ARTFUL EMBELLISHMENTS   III

Text and Crazy Quilts

Wording placed on a quilt can indicate names, places, and objects.

It's fun to add words to a crazy quilt, whether to sign and date it, or for any other reason. Text can be applied in a number of ways including pens and crayons that contain dye, and with outline and other embroidery stitches.

Test pens and crayons on different fabrics to find those that work well. It is easier to write on some fabrics than others; smooth cotton works best.

Always heat-set any dye materials that are used.

To embroider words, first sketch them onto paper and then use the Tracing Paper Transfer Method (see page 32). Ideas for words to place on a quilt:

Names of people and pets
Poetry
Quotes
Names of cities, states, countries
Words relevant to the theme of the quilt

Documenting a Quilt

Documentation is important if a quilt survives through many years. Many antique quilts were not signed and dated, making it difficult for historians to know anything of their history.

Your initials, the year the quilt is finished, and the city or state in which it is made are important bits of information.

You can include more information by sewing a pocket to the back of the quilt and inserting handwritten notes. These can be notes about the making of the quilt, any special fabrics that were used such as pieces of a wedding dress, any significance that the quilt has for you, and so on.

Chapter 4

Projects for Crazy Quilting

Small projects are a way to begin crazy quilting on a small scale before tackling a large project such as a quilt. Here are some special ideas to make for yourself or as gifts. Choose your own colors, threads, and embellishments to create your own work of art!

Method for Hooping Small Pieces

Embroidery and embellishing are easier to do if the project is in a hoop so that both hands are free to work. Here is a way to "hoop" a small project to fit it into a 14" lap hoop.

You will need some "throw-away" fabric. Either buy some on-sale, outdated quilting cotton, or some inexpensive muslin, or use something from your stash that you don't want for anything good. Have the project patched and basted, and ready for embroidery.

Cut a piece of the throwaway fabric a few inches larger than the hoop. Lay it flat. Place the project on top, centering it. Staying within the seam allowance, baste the project to the fabric, using short stitches. Turn the piece over, and carefully cut away the area of the throwaway fabric that is behind the project. Try to cut along the line of the seam allowance.

Place into the embroidery hoop, embroider and embellish. When finished, remove the basting stitches. The throwaway fabric can be reused if the newer project is larger all around than the first one.

A small project is hooped and ready for embroidery and embellishing.

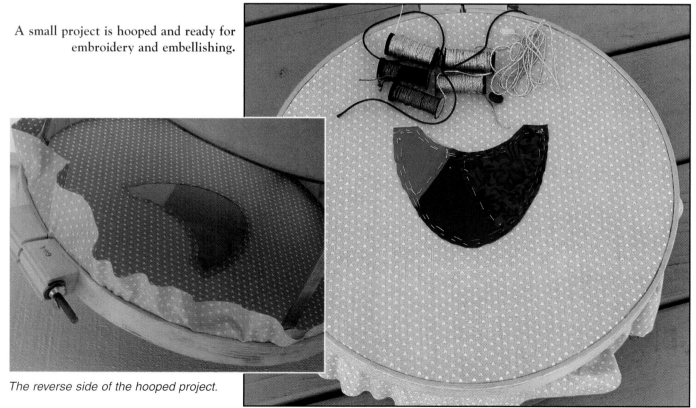

The reverse side of the hooped project.

A beaded fringe adds swingy piz-zazz to this crazy quilted neckpiece. Elegant for any special occasion, or wear with a denim shirt for a west-ern look.

Materials

Same size as pattern:
Silk organza for foundation
Silk fabric for backing
Cotton batting
Tracing paper, pencil, scissors
Small scraps of light-weight silk fabrics for patches
Kreinik metallic cords, braids, ribbons, Facets™ trim
Assorted glass seed beads
Metallic and/or rayon trims
½ yard rayon cording for edging
1 hank of size 11 seed beads, nylon beading thread, beading needle
Small quantity of size 6 or 8 seed beads
³⁄₁₆" cotton welting, black silk fabric to make bias silk tubes
4 split rings
Clasp

Necklace

A mélange of jewel-like materials atop a crazy quilted piece in silks. Assemble a small stash of silk fabrics, metallic threads and trims, and beads to make an elegant beaded neckwear piece. This one is made with a silk tube neckpiece, although a chain or beaded strand may be used instead. Use ¼" seam allowance.

Instructions:

1. Trace the pattern, cut it out, and cut out the fabrics as indi-cated. Patch the organza using the silk fabric scraps. Baste. Embroider and embellish using the Kreinik metallics, assort-ed seed beads, and metallic or rayon trims until the piece looks complete.

2. Trim away the seam allowance from the batting. Place the batting on the back and very lightly tack it to the foundation fabric so it is held in place.

3. Place the backing right sides together with the crazy quilted piece, and stitch around using a zipper foot. Leave an opening to turn. Turn right side out and carefully press.

4. Handstitch the cording all around, begin-ning and ending by concealing ends in the opening. Stitch the opening closed.

5. To make the beaded fringe, thread a beading needle with

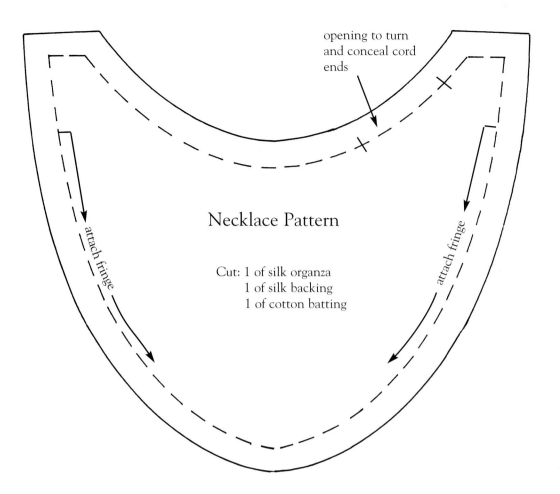

opening to turn
and conceal cord
ends

attach fringe

attach fringe

Necklace Pattern

Cut: 1 of silk organza
1 of silk backing
1 of cotton batting

about a yard of beading thread and fasten into the backing fabric at one end of the fringed area. Secure all thread ends by making several tiny stitches in the backing just under the edge of the cording. String on 3" of size 11 seed beads, one size 6 bead, then one seed bead. Ignore the final seed bead, and run the needle back through all of the remaining beads. Stitch into the backing, then run the needle through the fabric to the next fringe placement. Repeat. Make the fringes at regular intervals, about ³⁄₁₆" up to ¼" apart.

6. Stitch a split ring to each upper point of the piece. Make two fabric tubes.

Fabric tubes: hold the neckpiece up to yourself and measure to determine the length to make the fabric tubes. Cut a piece of welting the same length. Then cut the welting in half to have two equal pieces. Cut two pieces of silk fabric the same length as the weltings by about 1½" wide. Press under one long edge of the silk about ¼", roll the silk around the welting and slip-stitch, working into the folded edge. Carefully trim about ¼" of the cotton welting from each end of each tube. To finish the ends, turn in the bias and neatly hand-stitch. Stitch one end of each tube to the split rings on the necklace. Stitch split rings to the other ends of the tubes. Attach a clasp.

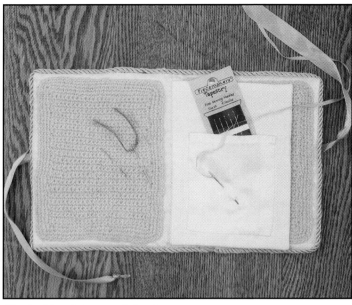

Fancy and practical, keep your needles organized in this silk crazy patched needlebook.

The inside of the needlebook.

Materials

11½" x 7½" white cotton fabric for backing

11½" x 7½" thin batting

11½" x 7½" muslin for foundation

11" x 7" smooth cardboard, ruler, pencil, craft knife, wide clear packaging tape

Small pieces of hand-dyed silk fabrics for patches

Embroidery threads

Embellishments of your choice

Small amount of "greasy" hand spun wool, approx. fingering weight, and a crochet hook to match the size of the yarn OR 2 pieces of wool felt, each 5" x 6½"

Two 5¾" x 7" white cotton fabrics

Two 11" lengths of ¾" wide satin ribbon, and two ¾" buttons

Needlebook

Here is a place to keep your needles handy, all in one place, and organized. The needle "pages" are crocheted out of handspun lanolin-rich wool to keep the needles clean and rust-free. You can do the same if you are able to obtain a small amount of wool yarn that was spun "in the grease." If not, wool felt can be used instead. This book is made with a piece of cardboard inserted so it feels like a covered book. There is a center "page" that is intended to protect the needles on both sides of the book and keep them from tangling. In this, if you like, stitch on a pocket or two for keeping packages of needles as they are purchased. Create your needlebook to suit your needs! Use ¼" seam allowances.

Instructions:

1. Patch the muslin with the hand-dyed silk fabrics using the Antique Method, and baste. Hoop the piece (see page 113), then embroider and embellish as you like. Layer: the crazy quilted piece right side up, the batting, and the white cotton backing right side down. By machine and using a zipper foot, sew around, leaving one end open. Turn right side out and press.

2. Take the cardboard, pencil and ruler. Find the center of the cardboard and draw a line. Draw two more lines on either side of the center, ¼" away. Erase the center line. With the craft knife, cut along the two lines. Keeping all the pieces butted together, apply packaging tape to hold them together. Tape one side only. This allows the book to fold while keeping the cardboard pieces together. Trim away a small amount from all four sides of the cardboard, just enough so it will fit, then insert the cardboard between the batting and the backing of the sewn piece. The taped side should face the interior of the book.

3. Fold in and press the seam allowances of the open end. Handstitch the end closed, leaving a small area unsewn to insert the cording ends. Slipstitch cording to the outer edge of the book concealing the ends in the opening. Sew the opening closed.

4. Crochet two pieces each 5" wide by 6½". (Or cut two pieces of wool felt.) Invisibly handstitch each piece to the cotton backing. If using hand-crocheted wool, stitch all around. If using wool felt, stitch at the top only, so the felt lifts up for inserting needles.

5. With right sides together, sew together the two remaining pieces of cotton fabric leaving an opening to turn. Turn and press, and then slipstitch the opening closed.

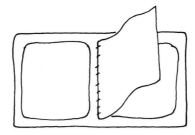

Handstitch the "page" to the center of the needle book. Optional: sew a pocket onto one or both sides of this page to store carded needles.

6. To make ties, gather one end of a satin ribbon and sew to the front of the book. Sew the other ribbon to the back of the book. Cover each stitching with a button. Tie a knot about 1" from the loose end of each ribbon, and fray the ribbon up to the knot.

Pillow

Pillows are easy to make and are a marvelous way of displaying a singular block of crazy quilting. The following pattern can be made the size of your choice. Before beginning the pillow top, purchase a pillow form and then make the pillow to fit. The one shown here is 18" square. It is backed with rose-colored cotton velveteen, and edged with a heavy cotton fringe. Use ½" seam allowances.

This pillow features a knife-edge finish, with cotton fringe sewn into the seam.

Instructions:

1. Patch the foundation according to the method of your choice. Embellish and embroider.

2. Cut the backing fabric in half, then hem each cut edge folding in ¼" twice, then sew along the folds.

3. With right sides together, pin the edging around the pillow top, neatly finishing the raw ends.

4. With right sides together, pin the backing pieces to the pillow top matching side, top, and bottom edges. The backing will overlap in the center of the pillow. Sew all around. Turn right side out and press. Insert the pillow form. Sew on hook-and-loop tape or snaps to the overlapping edges of the backing.

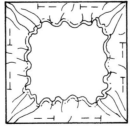

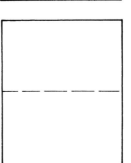

Materials

Pillow form the desired size

Muslin for foundation, the same size as the pillow form plus 1" each way for seam allowances

Backing fabric the size of the foundation plus an extra 6" in one direction.

Edging of your choice (optional), sufficient yardage to go around the pillow

Patch fabrics in 8 or more colors

Size 8 pearl cotton in 8 or more colors

Trims, laces as desired

Hook-and-loop tape, or snap closures

Sewing thread

Silver buttons, touches of leather, beads, and the colors of turquoise and old leather give this bag a Western look. Beaded feather stitching adorns the seams of Confetti piecing. Embroidery threads are Vikki Clayton's hand-dyed Silk Perles.

One way to adapt the purse pattern, this little number in black velveteen features rounded bottom corners, and only the flap is crazy quilted. Sewing buttons through all layers attaches the sewn velveteen strap.

Purse

Small purses are easy to make—you will want to make several for yourself and gifts. Adapt the design as you wish, note the flap variations as given in the diagram below. Choose fabrics and colors according to the intended uses of the purse (evening or casual). Also feel free to adapt the size of the bag—it can be made larger or smaller—any size you like. To make the strap, recycle an old leather belt, or sew a fabric strap or use cording. Use ¼" seam allowances.

Materials
Paper, pencil, ruler, scissors

8 cotton fabrics (see Confetti Piecing, page 25)

¼ yard of cotton fabric for lining

¼ yard of muslin

¼ yard of stiffener (heavy interfacing, buckram, etc.)

1 yard of cording

Embroidery threads

Embellishments of your choice

A handful of fancy and plain buttons

⅞" to 1" shank button for closure

2 metal loops

Strap (see instructions)

Sewing thread

Instructions:

1. Follow the diagram to make a paper pattern (tape sheets of paper together if needed). See the flap variations as diagrammed, and shape the flap as you wish. Use the pattern to cut out one each of muslin, lining, and stiffener.

2. Use the Confetti Piecing Method and the eight cotton fabrics to sew a piece the same as the pattern. Place the muslin on the back of the confetti piece. Baste all around. Hoop the piece (see page 113); embroider and embellish as you like.

3. Stack: the confetti piece right side up, stiffener, and backing with right side down. Machine sew around, leaving an opening to turn. Turn, press, and hand-stitch the opening closed.

4. Fold the purse front up to the fold line of the flap. Securely slipstitch both side seams.

5. Turn the purse inside out and form the bottom corners by matching the side seam with the center line of the bottom. Sew across the

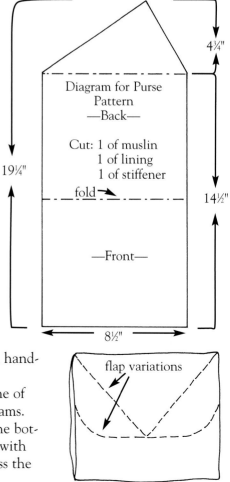

19¼"

4¾"

Diagram for Purse Pattern
—Back—

Cut: 1 of muslin
1 of lining
1 of stiffener

fold ➤

14½"

—Front—

8½"

flap variations

triangular area that forms, stitching about 1" in from the point. Turn the purse right side out.

6. Handstitch cording along the side seams and around the flap, forming a loop on the flap to fit the closure button, and leaving excess cording at each bottom edge. Tie a knot at each bottom edge, and fluff the ends for tassels.

7. Sew on a cluster of buttons along with the closure button. Add other buttons here and there on the purse to "tie" the layers.

8. Sew the metal loops to the upper corners and add a strap. Cut a narrow leather belt in half and stitch it onto the metal loops. You will need to punch holes in order to stitch through the leather. Use an awl, a leather punch, or a hammer and nail.

Scissors Holder

Wearing your scissors around your neck is more than a convenience. If you always return the scissors to the holder, it will always be handy. And, the holder looks like a fancy pendant. Make it like a piece of jewelry by adding a beaded neckpiece to the holder, and a beaded fob to your scissors.

The holder features a leather lining. Use a soft, light-weight leather that can be handstitched. This scissors holder is made for a 3½" scissors. Adjust the pattern as needed to accommodate your own embroidery scissors. ¼" seam allowances.

Instructions:

1. Trace the pattern, cut it out, and cut out the fabrics and leather as indicated.

2. To make the scissors holder front, patch the muslin using the hand-dyed fabrics. Hoop the piece (see page 113), then embroider and embellish as you like.

3. By machine, sew a lining to each of the front and the backing pieces, sewing all around. Cut a slit in the center of each lining and turn right side out, press. Stitch the openings closed.

4. Cut away the seam allowances from the leather pieces. Handstitch one leather to the upper edge of the front, and the other to the upper edge of the back, working between the dots. Keep the stitches tiny, and sew into the very edge of the leather.

Then, trim away just a small bit more from the unsewn edges of the leather pieces. This is so the leather will fit easily inside the fabric part of the holder. Handstitch the leather pieces together all around (with wrong sides together), stitching into the edges of the leather and keeping the stitches as small as possible.

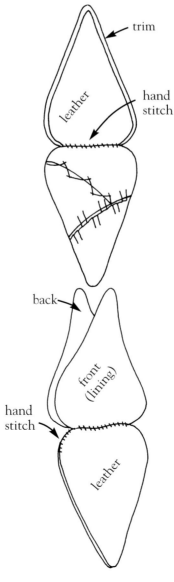

trim

leather

hand stitch

back

front (lining)

hand stitch

leather

This handy little number is fashioned of silk fabrics and light-weight leather.

Materials
Small amounts of:

Muslin

Light-weight silk fabric for lining (use anything—this lining will be enclosed)

Silk fabric for backing

Light-weight leather

Tracing paper, pencil, scissors

Hand-dyed silk fabric scraps

Cording (see instructions)

Embroidery threads and embellishments of your choice

Two bone rings

Sewing thread

Neckpiece (see instructions)

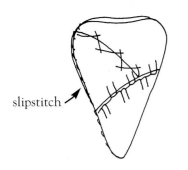

slipstitch

5. Fold the front and the back down over the leather pouch, and invisibly slipstitch the front to the back along the seams, enclosing the leather pouch.

6. Add a corded edging. Use a ready-made cording or twist, or braid threads together to make your own. Leaving a few inches at the bottom for a tassel, handstitch the cording to the edge of the holder, going around the entire front piece of the holder, and ending at the bottom. Tie the strands in an overhand knot, and fluff them to make a tassel.

7. Sew the bone rings to the upper edges of the scissors holder. Make or purchase a neckpiece. Use cording, string some beads, or attach a chain to the bone rings. Beaded scissors fob and neckpiece: check with your crafts store for beading supplies. String 6" of beads for the fob onto tiger tail, using crimp beads to secure the ends. The neckpiece can be strung onto tiger tail or beading thread. Make it about 24" long, adding a clasp if desired.

Scissors Holder Pattern

Cut: 1 of muslin
2 of lining
1 of backing
2 of leather

A Special Pillow

This special pillow is made of created fabrics. Its six patches are "fabrics" made of needlepoint, crochet, weaving, organza sandwich, punchneedle, and buttons. You can do the same as I did, or use your own skills to create unique patches. Assemble your created patches on muslin, then add embroidery and embellishments as you like.

This one is made very small to be displayed on a bookshelf. Make your pillow any size you like, from very small to large. This is your special pillow, so choose patch ideas, colors, and embellishments that have meaning or are special to you. ¼" seam allowances.

This pillow is intended to be a small, special piece, but the same concept could be used to create a larger pillow.

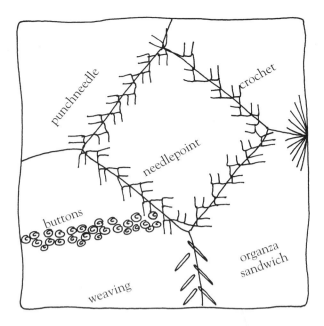

Even the backing fabric should be special; this is made of a silk/linen blend, and has a small hand-sewn pocket to store a small selection of thoughts, feelings, and info about the pillow.

Instructions:

1. Make the individual patches and arrange them on the muslin. Baste. Hoop the piece (see page 113), then embroider and embellish as you like.

2. Place the pillow top and backing with right sides together. Machine sew around, leaving an opening to turn. Turn, press, and stuff the pillow. Sew the opening closed.

3. To make the edging, thread a large needle with three strands of pearl cotton. Make a small stitch into the seam at the edge of the pillow. Cut the threads to about 3½" long, fold in half, and tie them into an overhand knot. Repeat around the pillow.

4. To make the pocket, turn in the upper edge of the 4" square of backing fabric and hem. Fold in the remaining three edges, pin, and slipstitch to the pillow backing.

Weaving:

Either purchase or make a small, simple loom. To make a loom, pound finishing nails into a small pine board. String the warp with a sturdy thread such as pearl cotton. Thread a long, dull needle with an embroidery thread and then weave back and forth. Finish all thread ends as you go by weaving them in a short ways.
Use a comb to keep the weaving snug. When finished, cut the warp threads.

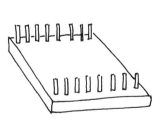

Materials

Threads and other materials for making your special patches

6½" square of muslin

6½" square of backing fabric

4" square of backing fabric for pocket

Threads and embellishments as desired

Stuffing

Size 8 pearl cotton for fringed edging

Needlepoint

I used Silk Serica thread on 18-count canvas. Use a tapestry needle that fits your thread, and a thread or yarn that covers the canvas well. Work in a slanted stitch, or cross stitch. Doodle on graph paper to come up with a geometric or other type of design. Finish the needlepoint, then trim the canvas to about ¼" from the edge of the stitching. Fold the edges under and press.

Organza Sandwich

See instructions on page 82.

Punchneedle

Lay a plain patch onto the muslin foundation. After the muslin is all patched and basted, draw a design on the back of the foundation behind the patch. Work the entire patch in punchneedle, filling it in completely. I used one strand of silk floss and a very fine punchneedle. See instructions on page 87.

Buttons

Lay a patch of plain fabric onto the muslin foundation. After the muslin is all patched and basted, sew on lots of buttons until the patch is entirely covered. They should overlap onto each other. I used mother-of-pearl buttons for their unique luster.

Crochet or Knit

The crocheted patch was made of single crochet in size 8 pearl cotton using a size 7 crochet hook. You can also knit a patch if you like, using a very fine yarn or thread. Make the piece the same shape as the desired patch.

There are nine paintings-on-fabric in this vest. Laces and embroideries create additional highlights against a background of hand-dyed plus black-and-white silk fabrics. Embroidery is worked in Vikki Clayton's hand-dyed Spun Silk Perle and Kreinik's Silk Serica threads, and YLI silk ribbons.

Vest

A vest is an easy project if you are familiar with basic garment sewing. If not, use the simplest pattern you can find, and follow the instructions carefully.

Choose a commercial pattern that has a fit that you like with no darts, pleats, or tucks so that all pieces are flat. Avoid buttonholes unless you plan carefully so they can be made in plain areas of patches.

Pick colors that you like to wear and add some neutrals such as black, white, gray, and brown. The pattern for the vest shown here is a "princess" style; all pattern pieces are flat, and the garment is shaped by the many shaped seams. There are four pieces for each of front and back, which may seem like lots of pieces, but each seam creates shaping for the garment.

Instructions

1. Cut the foundation fabric to the same size as the pattern. NOTE: if your patching and embroidery have a tendency to shrink the piece, cut the foundation slightly larger to accommodate this. Trim the foundation to the size of the pattern before assembling the vest.

2. Prepare several patches with acrylic paintings, in the designs of your choice. Patch the foundation using the Antique Method or the method of your choice, using the painted fabrics as some of the patches and adding laces into many of the seams. Work embroidery along patch seams and add any additional embellishments desired. Hoop the pieces if needed (see page 113) to prevent bunching.

3. Sew the vest, and add the lining according to pattern instructions. For a neat finish, add welting into the seams of the outer edges of the vest, or a cording may be hand-sewn on after the vest is assembled.

4. Tie the layers by sewing on buttons here and there, making tiny stitches, or using the method of your choice.

Materials

Vest pattern with flat pieces and a lining

Muslin for foundation, yardage as per pattern

Fabric for lining, yardage as per pattern

Silk fabrics for patches, including hand-dyed silks

Acrylic paints

Laces

Any desired embellishments

Threads for embroidery, silk ribbons

Sewing thread

Chapter 5

Finishing Touches

The 1898 quilt shown here is one of many crazy quilts bordered and backed with cotton sateen fabric. This quilt has a wool batting. Collection of the author.

Straight stitch fans decorate the velvet border of the 1862 "White Rose" crazy quilt. Detail. Photographed at Shiretown Antique Center, Alfred, Maine.

Note: This chapter gives several methods for finishing a crazy quilt, so read through to find what is most appropriate for your quilt project.

The variety of ways antique crazy quilts are assembled is yet another demonstration that this type of quilt was a creative phenomenon. Made with or without battings, the Victorian crazy quilted tops were finished with borders, bindings, laces, ruffles, or other edgings. They were tied with embroidery or sewn stitches, pearl threads, ribbons, and sometimes not tied at all.

Feather and herringbone stitches were used along block seams on this antique wool crazy quilt. This quilt was finished without a border. Owned by Avalon Antiques, photographed at Arundel Antiques, Arundel, Maine. Photo by Paul Baresel.

Adding a Border

Borders on some of the antique crazy quilts were extravagantly done, with corner fans, paintings on velvet, embroidery, ribbonwork, patchwork, appliqué, and other techniques. Even plain velvet borders have much to offer, adding a softening touch. Borders act as a frame, provide additional area to embellish, and expand the size of the quilt. Borders are sewn onto the quilt after patch embellishment and embroidery are finished.

Fabrics for Borders

Cotton sateen must have been considered a "utilitarian" fabric in the late 1800s. It was used for backings and borders on many crazy quilts, and also for vest linings and other uses. Its weight, satin surface, and elegant drape make it a perfect choice for finishing a quilt.

Many other fabric types also make excellent borders including velvet, velveteen, satin, silk noil and dupioni, bengaline, moire, damask, linens, and wools. Consider the fabric's weight, drape, fiber content and care features, and be sure it will be suitable for any embellishment method that you use.

You may need to try several different colors of fabrics to find the one that works best. Lay the quilt top onto a fabric and step back to see what it does for the quilt. Try several different fabrics and compare how they look with the quilt top.

Use black or dark colors for a border that will visually "recede," highlighting the quilt. A neutral color will enlarge the quilt without significantly changing its color scheme. If you choose a color similar to those in the quilt, you may wish to add a narrow contrasting sashing (as in the Butterstamp quilt).

Determining Yardage

For a small quilt, the borders can often be cut across the width of the fabric. In this case, the amount of fabric to buy is the width of a border times four. For larger quilts, cut the border from the length of the fabric. Purchase the length of fabric required for the longest border piece. Always purchase a little extra to allow for shrinkage and seam allowances.

Seam Allowances

Use your preference of a ¼" or ½" seam allowance. A ½" seam allowance adds 1" to the width, and 1" to the length of the quilt top, backing, batting, and border pieces. A ¼" allowance adds ½".

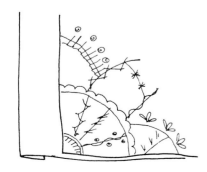

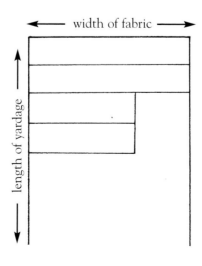

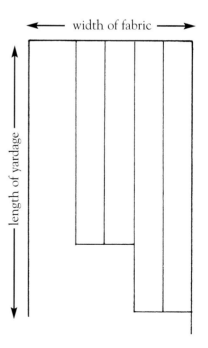

Interfacing the Border

For the border to hang properly, interface it with the same fabric used for the foundation of the quilt. Cut the foundation fabric the same as the borders, place them wrong sides together, and handle the two as one.

Pressing the Seams

If embroidery will be worked along the seam between border and quilt top, press this seam open. If not, press the seam toward the border.

A Plain Border

Determine the width of the border including seam allowances. To purchase yardage, two borders will equal the length of the quilt top, and two will be the width of the quilt plus two border widths.

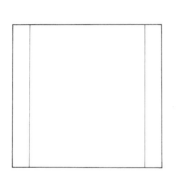  

Instructions

1. Measure the length of the quilt. Cut two borders this length. Back them with foundation fabric (see "Interfacing the Border" above). Sew one border to each side of the quilt.
2. Measure the width of the quilt including the side borders. Cut two borders this length, and back them with foundation fabric. Sew one to the top, and the other to the bottom of the quilt.

A Border with Corner Blocks

Make this the same as the plain border above, except make two borders the same length, and two the same width as the quilt top. Sew on the side borders. Make four corner blocks. Sew one corner to each end of the top and bottom border pieces then sew to the quilt top.

A border made with corner blocks is one of many ways that antique crazy quilts were finished. This one is edged with gold cording. Detail of an 1885 crazy quilt. The Brick Store Museum, Kennebunk, Maine.

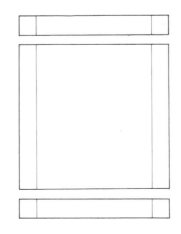 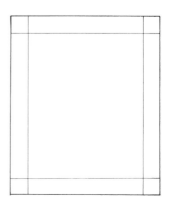

A Border with Mitered Corners

Determine the width of the border. To purchase yardage, two borders will equal the length of the quilt top plus two border widths. The other two will equal the width of the quilt plus two border widths. Cut out the borders. Back them with foundation fabric (see "Interfacing the Border," left).

Instructions

1. Sew each side border to the quilt top leaving the quilt's seam allowance unsewn at each end. Press the seams. Repeat to add the top and bottom borders.

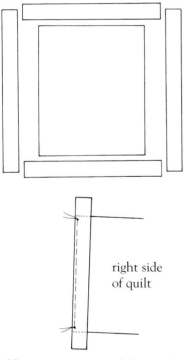

right side
of quilt

2. Place one corner of the quilt on the ironing board. Fold back the two adjoining borders, and make a crease exactly where the seam will be. Repeat for the remaining three corners.

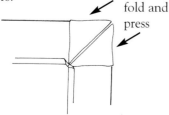

fold and
press

3. To sew each corner: with right sides together, line up the crease of each border section and pin. Sew from the outer edge to the inner edge. Trim away the excess fabric, and press the seam open.

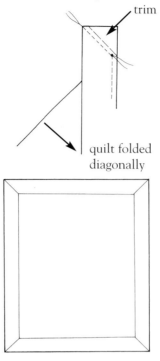

trim

quilt folded
diagonally

Embroidered or Appliquéd Border

Before adding the backing, work any embroidery or appliqué design as desired.

An unusual application of crazy quilting, the backing of this antique wool quilt was crazy patched of black fabrics and embroidered with bright threads. The red stitches are quilting stitches used to join the layers. Detail. Courtesy of the Kirk Collection, Omaha, Nebraska. Photo by Nancy T. Kirk.

Backings

The backing can be almost any good fabric. If the quilt will be finished with a knife-edge, you may want the backing to match the border. Measure the quilt, and if it is the same width (or less) than the width of the fabric, simply purchase the length needed. If the backing is to be pieced, purchase the quilt's length multiplied by two, and sew the backing with a vertical seam. As with the border fabric, buy a little extra to allow for shrinkage and seam allowances.

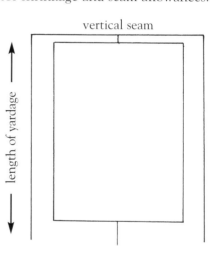

vertical seam

length of yardage

Battings

A batting can be added along with the backing after the quilt top is finished. Battings are entirely optional, and many Victorian crazies did not have them. The foundation fabric acts as a thin batting. If you want just a little extra thickness, use cotton flannel fabric for the foundation. For a thicker quilt, choose a cotton, wool, or synthetic batting.

Silk quilts can sometimes benefit from a little extra loft. Use a silk batting that can be pulled apart so you can add only the amount needed. It should be placed between two layers of silk fabrics. The silk fibers cling to each other holding the batting in place. When tying the quilt, work carefully to avoid the batting pulling out along with the tying threads. If this happens, trim the batting close to the quilt surface, and work it back inside.

This 1890s quilt is edged with a simple binding. Courtesy of the Kirk Collection, Omaha, Nebraska. Photo by Nancy T. Kirk.

Detail of the 1890s quilt. Courtesy of the Kirk Collection, Omaha, Nebraska. Photo by Nancy T. Kirk.

An antique block was formed into a pincushion in the shape of a pillow. A knife-edge finish offers a plain seam around the piece. Photographed at The Barn at Cape Neddick, Maine.

Knife-edge Quilt Finish

This is a simple way to add a backing. It creates an edge into which laces and trims may be inserted, and can be used on any quilt top, with or without borders.

Instructions

1. With right sides together, pin any lace or trim to the finished quilt top that will be sewn into the seam.

right side of quilt

Adding Gathered Lace or a Ruffled Edging

To make a gathered edging, begin with a length of lace or trim that is 1½ times the circumference of the quilt. Gather it by running a basting thread along the edge that will be sewn, and pin it with right sides together to the quilt top. Allow a few extra gathers at each corner of the quilt.

To make a ruffle, determine its finished width, add a seam allowance, and multiply times two. Cut bias strips this width (see How to Make Bias Binding, next page), and sew them together to make one long strip. Fold the strip in half lengthwise, gather, and pin with right sides together to the quilt top. Proceed with step two of the Knife-edge Quilt Finish.

2. Finish the ends of the trim by either sewing together the short ends, or overlapping and curving the ends outward so the raw ends will be sewn into the seam allowance.

3. With right sides together, place the backing fabric on the quilt top. If a batting is added, place it on top of the backing. Pin.

4. Sew around, leaving an opening to turn the quilt. Trim corners, and trim the seam allowance if necessary. Turn right sides out, press. Slipstitch the opening closed.

Binding

Binding is a traditional method of finishing a quilt that was sometimes used to finish Victorian crazy quilts. A binding can be used in place of, or in addition to a border.

Assemble the quilt layers with wrong sides together; quilt top, (batting if used), and backing. Pin and then baste around the outer edges. Measure around the quilt to determine the amount of yardage needed for the binding.

Instructions

1. Make or purchase sufficient double-folded, 1/2" wide bias binding.

right side
of quilt

2. Open out the binding and machine sew it with right sides together to the sides of the quilt top. Cut it even with the top and bottom edges of the quilt. Press, folding the bias to the back of the quilt. Pin, and invisibly slipstitch the folded edge of the binding over the seam.

back side
of quilt

3. Sew the bias to the top and bottom of the quilt, leaving at least ½" extra at each end. Fold in the ends neatly, press, and slipstitch as before.

How to Make Bias Binding

Choose a fabric for the binding. A plain cotton fabric is traditional and easy to handle, but other fabrics may be used instead such as silk, rayon, and even lightweight wool.

1. Begin with a square of fabric. A 36" square will yield sufficient bias for most quilts.

2. Fold the fabric diagonally as shown.

3. Press a crease along the fold then cut along it. Measure and cut strips. To make a ½" wide double-folded binding, cut the strips 1½" wide. This allows for ¼" seam allowances. For wider seam allowances, cut the strips wider.

4. Place the strips right sides together and sew ¼" seams as shown. Press the seams to one side.

5. To press the binding, first fold the strip in half lengthwise and press the fold. Then, turn in each long, raw edge ¼" and press. OR: use a bias tape maker to turn in the outer edges, then fold in two and press the center fold.

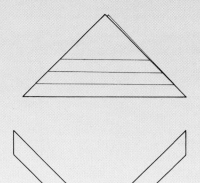

Tying the Quilt

After assembling the quilt, its layers are fastened together by adding ties. Here are some methods of tying that were used on Victorian crazy quilts. Choose one method, or combine several.

First, lay the quilt out flat on a clean floor or other surface that supports the entire quilt. Press it lightly if needed, and check that both sides lie smooth. If the quilt is large, safety-pin baste in a few places.

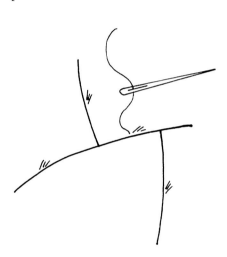

1. With sewing thread and needle, make small tacking stitches here and there over the entire top, having them about 4" apart or so. Place the stitches so they will be concealed by patch edges or embroidery.

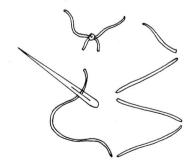

2. Thread a needle with a length of thread, pearl cotton, yarn, or ribbon and make small stitches about 5" to 6" apart. Cut the thread in between the stitches, and

tie the ends. Use square knots. It was customary to make these ties on the back of the quilt.

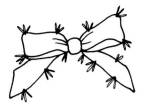

3. To conceal the ties, make small bows of ¼" to ½" wide ribbon and stitch them on top of the ties.

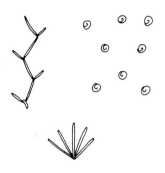

4. Add additional embroidery stitches to the face of the quilt, working them through all layers. Finish thread ends with a few tiny stitches (no knots) on the back. If the quilt has a batting, and before the layers are assembled, quilt the batting to the backing fabric with quilting stitches (short running stitch). Then add the quilt top, and tie in a few places.

Adding a Rod Pocket

To use a quilt as a wall hanging, add a rod pocket. Cut a strip of muslin or other fabric the width of the quilt by about 6" wide. To hem the ends, fold each short end under twice and sew. Press the long edges under about ¼", and slip stitch to the top of the quilt's backing. Place a dowel through the rod pocket to hang the quilt.

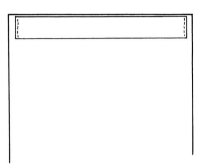

Detail of a vintage crazy quilt. Collection of The Brick Store Museum, Kennebunk, Maine.

Chapter 6

Gallery of Crazy Quilts

Instructions, or rather suggestions, are included for some of the quilts in this section. For greater detail, please refer to the specific instructions for patching, embroidery, and embellishments and finishing methods elsewhere in this book. Choose your own colors, size, and methods and do not focus on replicating any of the quilts exactly. Make it yours!

The Ladies and Fans quilt is all silk and features cigarette silks, silk ribbon embroideries, pieced fans, ribbon work, covered buttons, tassels, and a ruffled finish. The beautiful marbled silks in this quilt are the work of Ann Shurtleff of Pagosa Springs, Colorado.

All-silk Crazy Quilts

There is no comparison to the elegance of a silk quilt. Silk has a luxurious feel to it, and quilts made entirely of it are both lightweight and warm. The Victorians had sufficient quantities of this fabric, and made scrap quilts out of it. Silks appear in a great many antique crazy quilts. For everyone who makes crazy quilts, I heartily recommend making at least one all-silk quilt. You may never return to the other fibers!

Because it hand-dyes so easily, it is an easy thing to purchase say a yard of each of three or four different types of silk in white or off-white, and to hand-dye it in as many colors as you will ever need. See the Dye Experiments on page 103 as a way of easily developing a full color range.

Quilt size: 41½" wide x 42½" long, not including a 3" ruffle on three sides.

Materials

1½ yards of 42" wide silk organza fabric for foundation

Silk fabrics, commercially dyed and hand-dyed in a range of colors for patches

Basting thread

Cigarette silks (if available)

Several small paintings on silk

Silk ribbons in 4mm and 7mm, variety of colors

Wider silk ribbons to use as trims

Covered buttons (see page 82)

Small silk tassels (see page 80)

Twisted silk threads for patch seam embroidery

Silk batting (optional)

Silk fabric for ruffle (see Adding a Bias Ruffle, page 128)

1½ yards silk fabric for backing

Sewing thread

Ladies and Fans Silk Quilt

Pieced fans are found on many antique crazy quilts. They vary in size and shape, and were pieced of fabrics or ribbons. This all-silk wall quilt features five different fan designs. The quilt is finished in the style of a bed quilt with the ruffle placed on three sides only. Embellishments include cigarette silks, ribbonwork, silk ribbon embroideries, paintings, and embroideries. Many of the patches are hand-dyed.

With cigarette silks (or any antiques) in the quilt, it is a wall quilt and not intended to be used on a bed. I used the cigarette silks in this way to be able to preserve them and appreciate them at the same time.

Instructions

1. Begin with a square of organza fabric for the foundation, about 42" square. As you work on the organza, keep it "squared up" by using a table or cutting mat to be sure it is not skewed. Use the Antique Method of patching. Piece and add some fans as you do. On a quilt top of this size it is easiest to patch an area then do the pressing and basting before moving on.

2. After the quilt top is completely patched and basted, work embroidery along the patch edges. Use an embroidery hoop, or preferably, a lap hoop. Add any embellishments that you desire. Add cigarette silks by laying 7mm silk ribbon along their edges and tacking them lightly to the quilt. Take care that the cigarette silks do not become caught in the pinch of the embroidery hoop as you work on the quilt top.

3. When finished, add the quilt backing (see the chapter, Finishing Touches), and a thin layer of silk batting if you wish. Edge the quilt according to your preference, and add a rod pocket for hanging.

Silk Cocoon Jacket

Crazy quilted garments do not need to be heavy and bulky. This jacket—made of four layers of silk, patches, a thin batting, foundation, and lining—is nearly weightless. The cocoon style relies on drape for its elegant look, as do most oversized or loose-fitting garments. To achieve the maximum drape in a garment, use light, drapey silk patch fabrics, silk organza foundation, and a light- to medium-weight silk lining. Batting is optional. Choose a silk batting that can be pulled apart so that only a wispy layer can be used. Choose a commercial pattern that is a simple design with all flat pieces (no internal shaping such as darts or pleats), and no collar. Cut out a foundation for each pattern piece. Work crazy quilting on each. Assemble the garment according to pattern instructions.

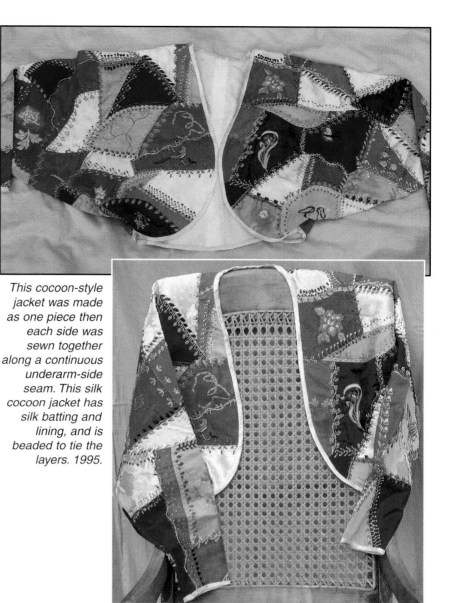

This cocoon-style jacket was made as one piece then each side was sewn together along a continuous underarm-side seam. This silk cocoon jacket has silk batting and lining, and is beaded to tie the layers. 1995.

When you first use a garment sewing pattern for crazy quilting, always take this time- and labor-saving step. Cut the basic pieces of the garment out of muslin or other inexpensive cotton fabric and sew them together. Try it on and make any necessary alterations or changes to the muslin. If there are changes, use the muslin as the pattern. By doing this you will be sure of the fit of the garment before all of the patching, embroidery, and embellishment commences.

A crazy quilted garment should be lined, so the ends of the many threads are all enclosed. This can be done in two ways. One is to choose a pattern that includes a lining. Assemble the garment according to pattern instructions.

If the pattern does not include a lining, make one by cutting lining pieces the same as the jacket pieces. Sew the lining seams and place the lining inside the sewn jacket with wrong sides together. Remove all seam allowances from the outer edges of both jacket and lining. Pin or baste along the edges to hold the layers. Finish the edges with bias binding (see How to Make Bias Binding on page 129).

Art Crazy Quilts

The term "art quilts" encompasses all types of quilting. They are a "follow your heart or artistic conscience" type of quilting, a description that easily includes most crazy quilts. Pushing the boundaries of crazy quilting can elevate the artistry involved.

The Piano Shawl shown "framed" demonstrates the draping potential of crazy quilts when they are made of materials that allow them to do so.

The Piano Shawl. 1996.

Landscape hanging. 1998. This small crazy quilted wall hanging incorporates ribbon work, cotton and rayon laces, and some painted patches.

Detail of the Piano Shawl.

The Piano Shawl

This quilt is made mostly of rayon challis fabrics, on a foundation of 100 percent cotton batiste. It features hundreds of French knots, my favorite embroidery stitch. Drape this quilt over a grand piano, or wear it to a party!

Unlike most of my quilts, this one includes some printed fabrics. The prints are embellished with embroidery. Ribbonworked flowers spill diagonally across the quilt. French knots profusely decorate the quilt and spill onto its border.

To make a similar shawl, choose your fabrics carefully, using those that are soft and drape beautifully. Make no substitutions for the rayon fringe; its sinuous drapeyness is the perfect finishing touch.

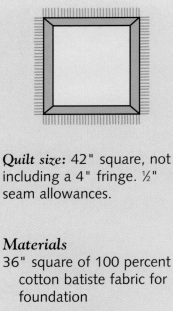

Quilt size: 42" square, not including a 4" fringe. ½" seam allowances.

Materials

36" square of 100 percent cotton batiste fabric for foundation

Rayon challis and other fabrics for patches

YLI Pearl Crown Rayon thread in 8 or more colors for embroidery along patch seams

Rayon ribbons, silk ribbons, laces, or other embellishments of your choice.

1¼ yards of silk or rayon fabric for backing

1½ yards of drapey rayon fabric (such as challis) for border

1½ yards of 100 percent cotton batiste for border interfacings

4¾ yards of 4"-wide rayon fringe

Instructions

1. Patch the cotton batiste foundation using either the Antique or Landscape Method, or a combination of both. Embroider along patch seams using Pearl Crown Rayon thread and variations of the outline stitch or the stitches of your choice. At the same time, add ribbonworked florals allowing them to flow across several patches. Think of unique ways to use ribbons so they mimic meandering plant forms.

2. See the chapter, Finishing Touches (page 124), to add a 3½" wide border with mitered corners, backing each border piece with batiste. Add a backing and the rayon fringe.

3. Tie the quilt by working meandering outline stitch on various patches.

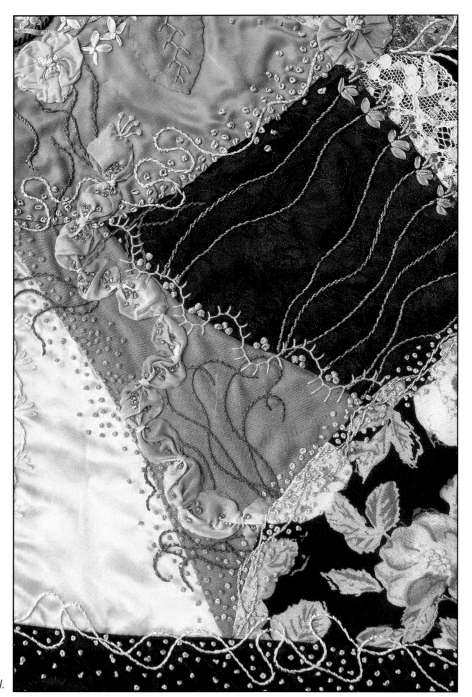

Detail of the Piano Shawl.

Crazy Quilts for Children

Until recent times, children were expected to learn adult skills including needlework. The small block shown here is a child's piece, on which she learned to patch, baste, and embroider. What better way to learn a variety of stitches!

This antique block is likely the work of a child learning to crazy patch and work embroidery stitches. In the center, a fan was attempted. Collection of Rocky Mountain Quilts, York Village, Maine.

Confetti Crib Quilt

Confetti piecing is a great way to quickly make a washable quilt. This quilt was completed in less than a day. Follow instructions for the Confetti Piecing Method (page 25), making the quilt in blocks or as one piece. See Finishing Touches, page 124, to add a border. Finish with a cotton batting, a backing, then bind the edges and tie the quilt.

Quilt size: 26" wide x 38" long.

A confetti-pieced crib quilt is displayed on a rocking horse made by the author's father, Ray Michler, and a cotton rug woven by the author's mother, Doris Michler. 1997.

The Cousins quilt is a family heirloom. 1997.

138 ❧ CHAPTER SIX ❧

The Cousins Quilt

The outline-stitched children on this twin-bed-size quilt are Kate Greenaway's Victorian-era drawings of children. These drawings are available as iron-on transfers published by Dover Publications (see Sources, page 158). Consider adapting this quilt to your own ideas. It would also be nice with embroideries or small paintings of antique toys.

The names and dates on this quilt are my son's cousins on the maternal side of my family, courtesy of my Aunt Elda who actively researches the family tree. The family is spread out from Oregon to Maine, and some of the names are cousins my son has never met.

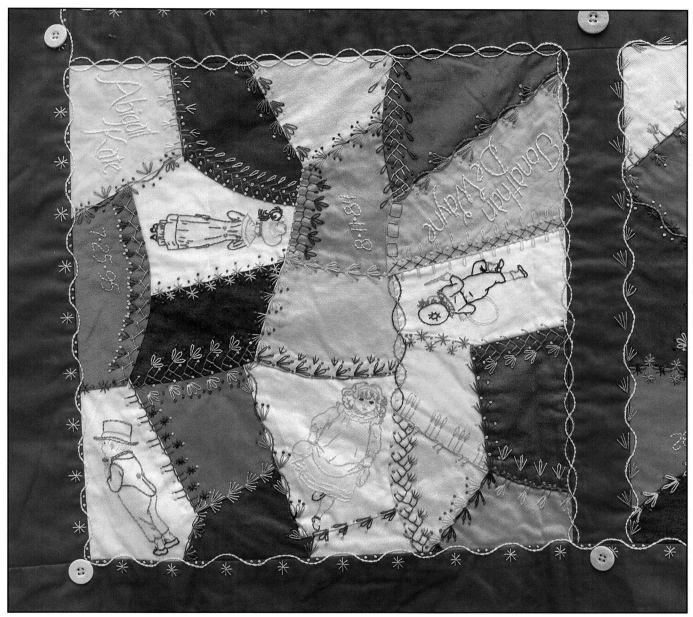

Detail of the Cousins quilt.

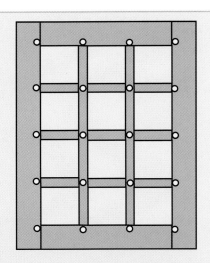

Quilt size: 62½" wide x 81" long. Use ½" seam allowances.

Materials

Twelve 16½" squares of muslin for foundations (or the size of your choice)

8 or more 100 percent cotton fabrics for patches: a mix of finishes including flannel, sateen, chintz, lightweight corduroy, etc.

2½ yards 100 percent cotton fabric for sashings and border

2½ yards muslin for border interfacings

Size 8 pearl cotton threads for patch seam embroidery, 8 or more colors

Size 12 pearl cotton or flower thread for embroideries in a variety of colors (or materials for your preferred method of illustration)

2½ yards 100 percent cotton fabric for backing

Self-made or purchased ½"-wide bias binding

Twenty ¾" 4-hole buttons

Sewing thread

Instructions

1. Patch the muslin squares in the Antique Method using the cotton fabrics. Make the patches large enough to add names, dates, and illustrations. With size 8 pearl cotton embroider along patch seams using two or three colors/stitches per seam. With size 12 pearl cotton or flower thread, embroider illustrations and names and dates.

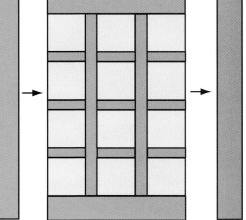

2. Arrange the blocks as they will be in the quilt. There will be three columns each with four blocks. Cut 3" wide sashings the same width as the blocks. Sew sashings between the blocks in each column. Press seams. Add two long sashings to connect the three columns. Press seams.

3. Embroider around each block using the stitches of your choice.

4. Following instructions in Finishing Touches (pages 124 to 126), add borders to the quilt top, cutting them 6" wide. Back the border pieces with muslin cut to the same size. With size 12 pearl cotton or flower thread embroider place names (such as cities or states) around the border.

5. The back of the quilt is constructed so that it can be taken apart easily to add additional names and dates:

Out of the backing fabric, cut out a second set of borders same sizes as for the front of the quilt. Lay them onto the back of the front borders, placing them the same, and baste to hold them in place. Finish the short ends by turning under and slipstitching.

6. Cut the backing so it will overlap onto the back borders at least 1" all around. Press the edges under and slipstitch to the quilt, without having the stitches come through to the front. Bind the outer edges of the quilt (see Binding, page 129). "Tie" the quilt by sewing buttons to the intersections of the sashings.

To add additional names and dates, simply open up the slipstitching around the backing, and take off any buttons in the area the embroidery will be worked.

Memory Quilts

The Victorian version of a memory quilt was a mourning quilt, made after a loved one passed on. Mourning crazies tend to be dark (made mostly of black fabrics), somber, and dismal looking. The memories evoked by these would be more significant of the grief of the mourner, rather than a celebration of the person now gone.

Now, we celebrate the happy memories, the good thoughts, the memorable moments by making a memory piece that in some way documents or reflects upon a person's life.

Detail of a Victorian mourning quilt. Collection of Rocky Mountain Quilts, York Village, Maine.

Shadowbox, a memory piece. 1998. The shadowbox frame was made out of an antique picture frame.

Memories of Grandmother, a Shadowbox

My paternal grandmother left behind crocheted laces, a black beaded necklace, and lots of memories—of her corn relish, her passion for gardening, her strength, and love of life. Photographs printed onto fabric are commonly found on memory quilts, but I chose to not include her visual image in this shadowbox. Here, velveteen was stenciled with a moon, tree, hollyhock, and fern, and embroidery was added.

To make a similar piece, begin with a shadowbox frame, and make a piece of crazy quilting to fit into it. Work the embroidery and embellishments of your choice then glue the piece into the frame. Add any additional objects, such as a small purse, necklace, hankie, or what have you, fastening them in with stitches or ties.

The Victorian Quilt

The first crazy quilt you ever make is a memorable experience from start to finish. It is an accomplishment of which you can be proud. Once finished, you will know that you can do it, and that is incentive to begin the next!

My first crazy quilt consists of a collection of small embroideries that were worked on scrap fabrics before being assembled into a quilt. Additional embellishments were added after the quilt was patched. The border consists of simple outline stitch embroidered stems and leaves with silk ribbon flowers worked on cotton sateen fabric.

The size of this quilt is ideal for both the whole quilt style (see page 19), and the beginner. It makes a good-sized wall quilt, but can also be used on a bed or over the back of a couch for decoration. Either assemble a quantity of patches with embroideries on them, or work embroideries on the patches after the quilt is patched.

Pattern for the border embroidery. Transfer the heavy line using the Tracing Paper Transfer Method (page 32).

Instructions

1. Patch the foundation according to the Antique Method using the patch fabrics, pre-made embroideries, photos on fabric, and laces. Embroider along patch seams using the pearl cotton threads. Embellish as desired.

2. Following instructions in the chapter Finishing Touches, cut out and sew on borders using the border style of your choice. Back the border pieces with muslin cut to the same size. See the diagram to work embroidery along the borders using the green pearl cottons and silk ribbon. First embroider a twining stem in Outline stitch around all borders. To make it stand out, embroider a second row of Outline stitch next to the first. Then, randomly add stems in a single row of Outline stitch. Make a silk ribbon flower at the end of each using a Lazy Daisy stitch with two Straight stitches for each. Randomly add leaves using the stitch of your choice.

3. Add the backing using the knife-edge method. Tie the quilt having the ties on the back.

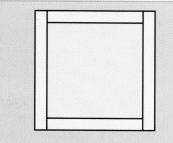

Quilt size: 54" x 52". The border is 4½" wide. 1/4" seam allowances.

Materials

45½" x 43½" muslin for foundation, or the size of your choice

Fabric scraps for patches: cottons, silks, acetates, etc.

Cotton laces

1½ yards of cotton sateen fabric for borders

1½ yards of muslin for border interfacings

1½ yards of fabric for quilt backing

Size 8 pearl cotton threads in 8 or more colors for embroidery

Embellishments such as buttons, beads, photos on fabric, cording, ribbon work, silk ribbon embroideries.

Sewing thread

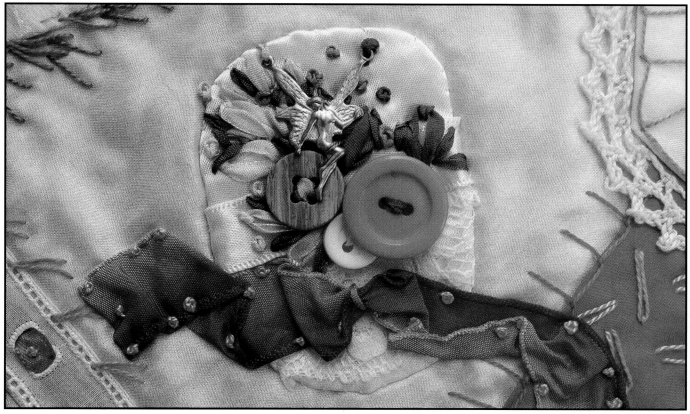

Detail of the Victorian quilt.

Miniature Crazy Quilts

Use miniature quilts as wall art, hanging them on a dowel as a wall quilt, or mat and frame them. Or, use them for other purposes such as pillow tops and doll quilts. Make the patches tiny, and the stitches very fine. A great way to use up small fabric bits!

Tiny silk patches are laid onto a silk organza foundation.

Doll's Quilt

Lightweight silk fabrics are ideal for miniature work since even the smallest patches are easy to work with. Crazy patch this fancy doll's quilt onto a silk organza foundation, then add a light layer of silk batting and a pretty lace ruffle. Such a quilt makes a wonderful gift for children of all ages who collect dolls! It can be made close to a 1:1 scale (1 inch = 1 foot) if the patches are made quite small.

Quilt size: 9" x 10" not including a 2¼" ruffle on three sides.

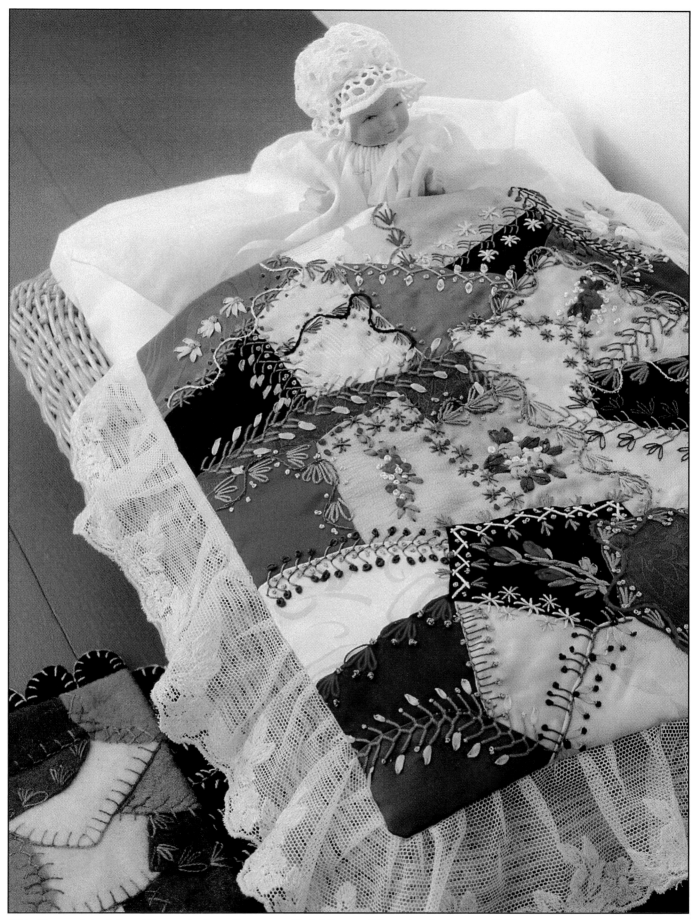

This 6" porcelain doll cuddles under her silk crazy quilt. A felt rug will keep her feet warm. 1997.

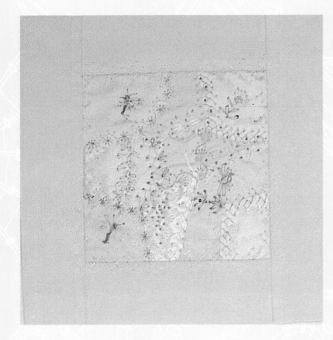
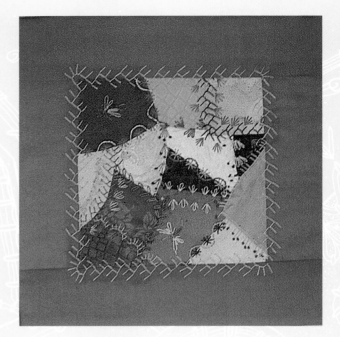

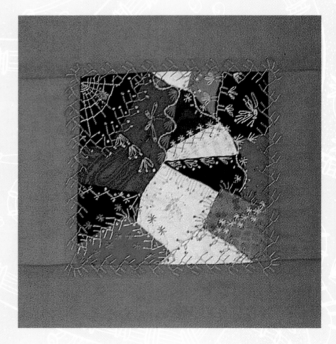

A set of four miniature crazy quilts. 1997.

Miniature Quilt

Miniatures are a great way to work out color scheme ideas. The small format makes it possible to complete a project in little time, so you can see how the colors work, and what embroidery does for the piece. They also make great gifts and wall decorations.

An optional way to finish the block is to mount it onto foamcore, place a mat on it, and frame the piece. For best results, see a professional framer.

Instructions

1. Patch the foundation using the Antique or Landscape Method. Hoop the piece (see page 113), and embroider. Remember to scale down the sizes of patches and embroidery stitches so that you are working in miniature. Add some embroidered insects or the embellishments of your choice.

2. Add borders (see the chapter, Finishing Touches), cutting the strips 2¼" wide. Work embroidery along the inner seams of the borders.

3. Add a knife-edge backing (page 128). Sew on a rod pocket for hanging (page 130), or have the piece professionally mounted and framed.

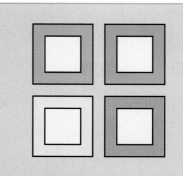

Quilt size: 8-½" square. ¼" seam allowances.

Materials

5½" square of foundation fabric (muslin, batiste, or organza)

Small pieces of silk fabrics

A fine, twisted thread in 8 or more colors, Silk Bella or Soie Gobelin

¼ yard of silk noil or dupioni for borders

9" square of silk fabric for backing

Sewing thread

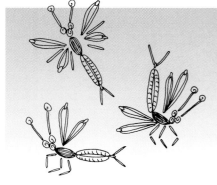

Embroidered Insects

Here are some tiny bugs to add to your miniature work. Use a very fine, twisted silk embroidery thread such as Silk Bella. Make two Bullion stitches side by side, then Padded Satin. Three French knots for the head, pistil stitch for antennae, lazy daisy for wings (wings can be worked in silk ribbon using the ribbon stitch). Add some legs of straight stitch.

Theme Crazy Quilts

Sometimes it is fun to create a quilt around a theme. Once you choose an idea, represent it by a central motif, as in the Victorian Horse quilt, or by adding appropriate embellishments. Appliqué, photo transfer, outline embroidery, words and quotes, painted details, are some ways to put your theme onto a quilt. Here are some ideas for subject matter:

- A favorite vacation spot or scene
- Cats, dogs, or other pets
- Sailing ships and nautical motifs
- Flowers, trees, herbs
- A sport
- Royalty, Egyptian pharaohs, other dignitaries
- Fairy tales, mythology, angels

The "White Rose" quilt is an example of an antique crazy quilt that has a theme. Detail. Photographed at Shiretown Antiques, Alfred, Maine.

The Victorian Horse Quilt was photographed in the garden just after the ice storm of January, 1998.

Victorian Horse Quilt

An old-fashioned horse toy theme makes this quilt suitable for a collector, a child's room, or a decoration in almost any room. The theme, framed by a crazy quilted border, is the central focus of the quilt.

The Butterstamp quilt is a theme quilt displaying folk art images. 1994.

The Butterstamp Quilt

Butterstamps and buttermolds often feature beautiful handcarved designs including florals, geometrics, cows, swans, initials, and others. The folk art stamps were once used to imprint a farm family's homemade butter.

To make this quilt, butterstamp images were transferred to silk fabrics using the "Rubbings" technique on page 111. A few words were also embroidered on including "butter prints," "antiques," "folk art," "Americana," and "Limerick." In keeping with the folk art images, an old-fashioned-looking patchwork border encloses the crazy patched area.

To make a similar quilt, choose a theme, and then decide how to represent it. Patch the quilt top, and finish with a narrow sashing and a patchwork border. Fabrics used here are cottons, velveteen, and silks. The border consists of cotton chintzes in colors that harmonize with those in the quilt.

Detail of the Butterstamp quilt.

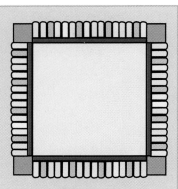

Quilt size: 56½" wide x 58¾" long. ¼" seam allowances.

Materials

2 yards of muslin for foundation and border interfacings

Fabrics for patches including cottons, velveteen, silks.

Rubbings (see page 111), or other images of your choice

Size 8 pearl cotton in 8 or more colors.

Small lace motifs

Strips of contrasting fabric for sashings (see instructions)

Assorted cotton fabrics for border

Paper, pencil, scissors

Instructions

1. Work rubbings on some of the silk patch fabrics following instructions on page 111.

2. Cut a muslin foundation 43½" wide x 45¾", or the size of your choice.

Patch the foundation using the silk rubbings and other patch fabrics. Add lace motifs to some of the patches. Baste. Embroider along patch seams using size 8 pearl cotton.

3. Scalloped border: Copy or trace the pattern onto plain paper and cut it out. Cut out the needed number of patches for the length of each border, and cut an equal number out of muslin. Place a muslin patch on the back of each patch and handle the two as one. Sew patches together to make each border. Press seams open.

4. Cut two sashings each 1½" wide by the length, and two the width of the quilt. Sew one to each patchwork border. Cut four corner blocks each 7¼" square, and sew one to each end of the top border. Do the same for the bottom border. Sew the side borders to the quilt, then the top and bottom borders.

5. Backing: Cut the backing slightly larger than the quilt, making it in two pieces (be sure to allow for the center seam allowances). Sew the center seam, leaving the middle of it unsewn so the quilt can be turned later. Press the seam open. Place the backing and quilt top right sides together, and pin carefully all around. Taking your time, sew carefully all around. End stitching at each patch seam, and begin stitching on the following patch without leaving a gap.

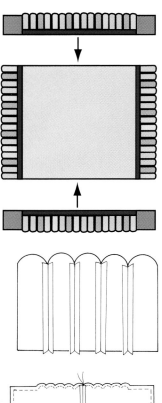

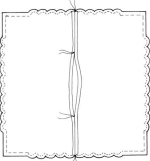

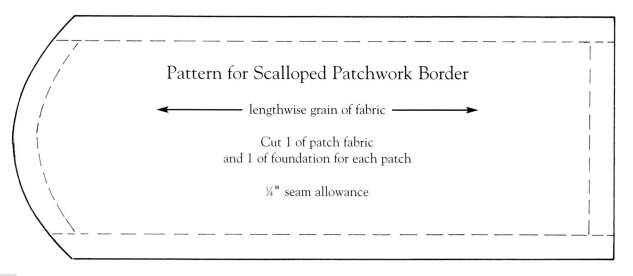

Pattern for Scalloped Patchwork Border

← lengthwise grain of fabric →

Cut 1 of patch fabric
and 1 of foundation for each patch

¼" seam allowance

6. Trim excess backing fabric, and trim seams. Turn the quilt right sides out, and carefully press the scalloped edges. Slipstitch the center of the backing closed.

7. Tie the quilt top, having the ties on the back. Work embroidery stitches along the sashings and the seams of the patchwork border.

A lap quilt in neutral shades will fit almost any home décor.

Wool and Country-style Crazy Quilts

Many Victorian crazy quilts were made of wool as a practical alternative to the fancy ones. These often feature very little fancy stitching, and many have appliqués or simple outline embroideries decorating the patches.

But even a wool quilt can be made fancy! Embroider the quilt using wool threads (see Wool Embroidery on page 97). Incorporate pieces of unfinished or small pieces of needlework if you have them. Crewel and needlepoint pieces worked in wool are especially compatible with wool quilts.

The Horses and Roses quilt draped, with the Folk Hearts quilt on the wall. Both are at home in a country-style setting.

Horses and Roses Wool Quilt

This large quilt is assembled of blocks to keep the work in manageable pieces. It is bordered with an appliqué design in wool, and edged with hand-crocheted lace. Shown here, it is only halfway finished, the doily on the red block later became the quilt's center. It is a fancy version of a wool quilt, featuring wool embroidery, and cross stitchings of horses, needlepoint, and appliqués. The needlework pieces contribute interesting textures that combine nicely.

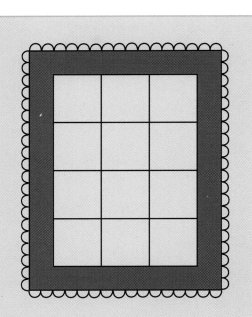

Quilt size: 73" wide by 93" long, not including the lace edging. The borders are 6" wide. ½" seam allowances.

Materials

5½ yards of 100 percent cotton flannel for foundation

Wool and other fabrics for patches, such as linen, velveteen, cottons

Cotton laces

Evenweave linen in various colors, cross stitch designs, embroidery flosses

Wool threads for embroidery

Materials for appliqué, punchneedle, other embellishments of your choice

5½ yards of 100 percent cotton fabric for backing

2¾ yards of wool fabric for borders

2¾ yards of muslin for border interfacings (if needed)

10 yards of light-green cording, and pieces of red, ivory, and green wool for border appliqués

9½ yards of 3"-wide hand-crocheted or other lace for edging

Sewing thread

Instructions

1. Cut the flannel into twelve 21" squares. Work cross stitch designs of your choice on the linen evenweave fabrics. Patch the foundation in the Antique Method using the cross stitch pieces and the wool and other fabrics. Add laces. Baste. Embroider (see "Wool Embroidery" on page 97). Work appliqués and punchneedle motifs on some of the patches.

2. Assemble the blocks into three columns each with four blocks. Sew the columns together. Press seams open. Work an embroidery stitch along the seams.

3. Using the border style of your choice, cut out and sew on the borders (see the chapter, Finishing Touches). Use a muslin interfacing if needed.

4. Meander the light green cording around the border and hand-stitch in place. See the diagrams to cut out flowers and leaves. Appliqué them (see Appliqué on page 77), and add embroidered details.

5. Add the backing using a knife-edge finish (see page 128). Handstitch the lace to the outer edges of the quilt, gathering at corners to turn the corners neatly.

Detail of the Horses and Roses quilt.

To press under the edges of wool patches, use a water-filled spray bottle and a dry iron. Place a press cloth over the wool, spray lightly, and press. The steam will set the crease. Allow the fabric to dry before handling the patch.

The Horses and Roses wool quilt. Shown unfinished.

Detail of the Horses and Roses quilt.

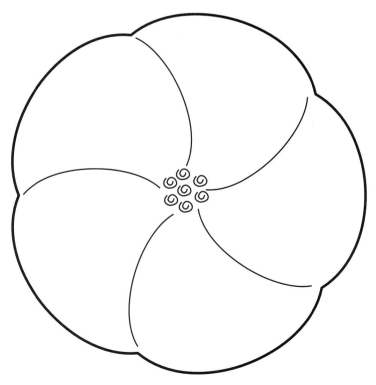

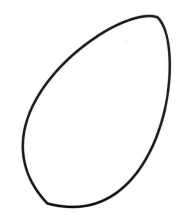

Actual-size diagrams for flower and leaf appliqués. Cut out as many as needed, adding seam allowances.

Fund Raiser and Commemorative Crazy Quilts

This fund raiser quilt was made by members of The Valley Needlers, South Hiram, Maine. 1997. Fund-raiser and commemorative crazy quilts are quilts made by groups rather than individuals. Quilts can be designed to celebrate anniversaries of local importance, such as the founding of a town or city, or made for the purposes of a charity. They are then raffled or auctioned off to raise funds. They can be made as theme quilts, with appliqués and embroideries showing items of importance, or not. The Valley Needlers Quilt Guild, members of the Maine State Pine Tree Quilter's Guild, Inc., made a crazy quilt for their annual raffle in 1997. Each block of the quilt was completed by a member of the group. The quilt was displayed at the Maine State Quilt Show, at several fairs and local events then raffled off with the proceeds used to benefit a local high school.

Since 1998, an annual fund raiser quilt (or two) has been made by
members of the Quiltropolis.com crazy quilt email list. These quilts were then
displayed at the annual Crazy Quilt Conference in Omaha, Nebraska, and raffled off.
Proceeds were donated to the American Cancer Society to benefit breast cancer research.
The full size quilt shown here is called the Millenium Quilt, and was made in the year 2000.
These three photos were taken by Kate Hollifield.

The Meanings of Flowers

The Victorians attached great importance to meanings given to flowers. These were used as a communication device by young lovers; in bouquets, and valentines, for example. Flowers hold meanings for love, death, general and religious purposes. In addition, herbs, trees and vegetables were given meanings.

Those listed here are excerpted from two books: The Bouquet: Containing The Poetry and Language of Flowers, by a Lady, published by Benjamin B. Mussey, Boston, 1846. This is a charming small book with gold edged pages, and a poem for each flower. The other is a hefty tome, titled Woman's World, A Complete Guide to Perfect Womanhood, by Mary Alice Sullivan, published by Monarch Book Co., Philadelphia, PA, 1894.

Use the flowers individually or in bouquets to combine meanings. Create secret "messages" on a crazy quilt! Or, choose a flower because of its meaning and make a theme quilt around the idea. Consult with flower encyclopedias and illustrated gardening catalogs for pictures of the flowers.

Flower	Meaning
Acacia, yellow	Concealed love
Aconite (Wolfsbane)	Misanthropy
Almond (Flowering)	Hope
Aloe	Religious superstition
Alyssum (Sweet)	Worth beyond beauty
Amaranth, Globe	Unchangeable, unfading love
Amaryllis	Pride, timidity, splendid beauty
Anemone	Anticipation
Angelica	Inspiration
Apple	Temptation
Arbor Vitae	Unchanging friendship, live for me
Auricula, scarlet	Wealth is not happiness
Bachelor's Button	I with the morning's love have oft made sport
Balm	Sympathy
Balsamine	Impatience
Basil	Hatred
Bay Leaf	I change but in dying
Belladonna	Silence
Betony	Surprise
Bluebell	Constancy
Borage	Bluntness
Box	Stoicism
Cabbage	Profit
Cactus	Warmth
Camellia, white	Perfect loveliness
Candytuft	Indifference
Canterbury Bell	Acknowledgment
Chamomile	Energy in adversity
China Aster	Variety is charming
Chrysanthemum, red	I love you
Clematis	Mental beauty
Cloves	Dignity
Columbine	I cannot give thee up
Coreopsis	Love at first sight
Corn	Riches
Cowslip	Pensiveness, winning grace
Crocus	Cheerfulness
Currant	Thy frown will kill me
Daffodil	Regard
Daisy	Beauty and innocence
Damask Rose	Brilliant complexion
Dandelion	Coquetry
Dew Plant	Serenade
Dogwood	Durability
Eglantine	I wound to heal
Endive	Frugality
Eupatorium	Delay
Everlasting	Always remembered
Fennel	Strength
Fern	Fascination
Flax	Domestic industry
Flowering Reed	Confidence in Heaven
Forget-me-not	True love
Foxglove	Insincerity
Geranium, Oak	True friendship
Geranium, Rose	Preference
Gilly Flower	Bonds of affection
Goldenrod	Precaution
Grass	Submission
Harebell	Grief
Hawthorne	Hope
Heath	Solitude is sometimes best society
Heliotrope	Devotion, faithfulness
Hibiscus	Delicate beauty
Hollyhock	Ambition
Honey Flower	My love is sweet and secret
Houstonia	Contentment
Hyacinth	Sport, game, play
Hydrangea	Heartlessness
Hyssop	Cleanliness
Ice Plant	Your looks freeze me
Iris	I have a message for you
Ivy	Wedded love
Jacob's Ladder	Come down to me
Japan Rose	Beauty is your only attraction
Jasmine, white	Amiability
Jonquil	I desire a return of affection
Laburnum	Pensive beauty
Lady's Slipper	Win me and wear me
Larkspur	Fickleness
Laurel	Glory
Laurustinus	I die if neglected
Lily, white	Purity and sweetness
Lily of the Valley	Delicate simplicity
Locust	Affection beyond the grave
Lotus	Eloquence
Love-in-a-mist	You puzzle me
Love Lies Bleeding	Hopeless, not heartless
Magnolia	Love of nature
Mallow	Mildness
Marigold, French	Jealousy
Meadowsweet	Uselessness
Mignonette	Your qualities surpass your loveliness
Mimosa	Sensitiveness
Mint	Virtue
Mistletoe	I surmount all difficulties
Monkshood	Chivalry
Morning Glory	Affectation
Myrtle	Love in absence
Narcissus, Poet's	Self-love, egotism
Nasturtium	Patriotism
Nightshade	Truth
Oats	Music
Oleander	Beware
Orange Blossom	Your purity equals your loveliness
Ox Eye	Patience
Parsley	Feasting, entertainment
Pansy	Tender and pleasant thoughts
Passion Flower	Religious fervor
Pasque Flower	You have no claims
Pea, Everlasting	Wilt thou go with me?
Pea, Sweet	Departure
Peach Blossom	I am your captive
Peony	Shame, bashfulness
Periwinkle, blue	Sweet remembrance
Phlox	Our souls are united
Poppy, red	Forgetfulness, or consolation
Poppy, white	Sleep of the heart
Primrose	Early youth
Primrose, Evening	Inconstancy
Queen's Rocket	You are the queen of coquettes
Quince	Temptation
Ranunculus	You are radiant with charms
Rhododendron	Danger, beware
Rose	Love
Rose, bridal	Happy love
Rose, moss	Superior merit
Rosemary	Remembrance
Rue	Disdain
Sage	Domestic virtues
Shamrock	Light-heartedness
Speedwell	Fidelity
Spiderwort	Esteem, not love
Star of Bethlehem	Light of our path
St. John's Wort	Animosity
Stock	Lasting beauty
Sunflower, dwarf	Your devout admirer
Syringa	Memory
Tansy	I declare war against you
Tuberose	Dangerous pleasures
Tulip, red	A declaration of love
Verbena	Sensibility
Veronica	Fidelity
Violet	Modesty
Wallflower	Fidelity in misfortune
Weeping Willow	Mourning
Witch Hazel	A spell
Woodbine	Fraternal love
Wormwood	Absence
Yarrow	Thou alone must care
Yew	Sorrow
Zinnia	Thoughts of absent friends

Selected Bibliography

Bond, Dorothy. *Crazy Quilt Stitches.* self published: 1981.

Brandt, Janet Carija. *Wow! Wool-on-Wool Folk Art Quilts.* That Patchwork Place, 1995.

Burchell, S.C, and The Editors of Time-Life Books. *Age of Progress.* NY: Time-Life Books, 1966.

Caulfield, S.F.A., Saward, Blanche C. *Encyclopedia of Victorian Needlework (Dictionary of Needlework),* Vols. 1 & 2. NY: Dover Publications, 1972. Unabridged republication of the second edition (1887) of the work originally published by A.W. Cowan, London in 1882 under the title *The Dictionary of Needlework: An Encyclopedia of Artistic, Plain, and Fancy Needlework.*

Chijiwa, Hideaki, *Color Harmony: A Guide to Creative Color Combinations.* MA: Rockport Publishers, 1987.

Christopher, Barbara. *Traditional Chinese Designs: Iron-on Transfer Patterns.* NY: Dover Publications, Inc., 1987.

Coats, J&P, Ltd. *The Anchor Manual of Needlework.* Interweave Press, 1990.

Conroy, Mary. *The Complete Book of Crazy Patchwork: A Step-by-Step Guide to Crazy Patchwork Projects.* NY: Sterling Publishing Co., Inc., 1985.

Dewberry, Donna. *Donna Dewberry's One Stroke Painting Course.* NY: Sterling Publishing Company, Inc., 1999.

Fanning, Robbie and Tony. *The Complete Book of Machine Embroidery.* Chilton Book Company, 1986.

Gardner, Pat Long. *Handkerchief Quilts.* Virginia: EPM, 1993.

Glazier, Richard. *Historic Textile Fabrics.* Great Britain, 1923.

Hasler, Julie S. *Kate Greenaway Iron-on Transfer Patterns.* NY: Dover Publications, Inc., 1990.

Haywood, Dixie. *Crazy Quilt Patchwork: A Quick and Easy Approach with 19 Projects.* NY: Dover Publications, Inc., 1986.

Hibbert, Christopher. *Queen Victoria in Her Letters and Journals, A Selection.* NY: Viking, 1985.

Horton, Laurel, editor. *Quiltmaking in America, Beyond the Myths.* Nashville, TN: Rutledge Hill Press, 1994.

Hulbert, Anne. *Folk Art Quilts: 20 Unique Designs from the American Museum in Britain.* London, England: Collins & Brown, Ltd., 1996.

Hubert, Carol. *An Introduction to Wool Embroidery.* Australia: Kangaroo Press, 1991.

Jarratt, Maisie. *French Embroidery Beading: How to Bead.* Australia: Kangaroo Press, 1991.

Kolander, Cheryl. *A Silkworker's Notebook.* Loveland, CO: Interweave Press, Inc. Revised edition, 1985.

Laury, Jean Ray. *Imagery on Fabric.* CA: C&T Publishing, 1992.

Laury, Jean Ray, John Cram, Liz Aneloski. *The Photo Transfer Handbook: Snap It, Print It, Stitch It.* CA: C&T Publishing, 1999.

MacColl, Gail, Wallace, Carol McD. *To Marry an English Lord.* NY: Workman Publishing, 1989.

Maisel Ph.D., Eric. *Fearless Creating: A Step-by-Step Guide to Starting and Completing your Work of Art.* NY: Tarcher/Putnam, 1995.

McMorris, Penny. *Crazy Quilts.* E.P. Dutton, 1984.

Michler, J. Marsha. *Ribbon Embroidery, with 178 Iron-on Transfers.* Mineola, NY: Dover Publications, Inc., 1997.

Montano, Judith B. *The Handbook of Crazy Quilting.* C&T Publishing, 1986.

- *Crazy Quilt Odyssey.* C&T Publishing, 1991.

Nichols, Marion. *Encyclopedia of Embroidery Stitches, Including Crewel.* NY: Dover Publications, Inc., 1974.

Nylander, Jane C. *Fabrics for Historic Buildings.* Washington, DC: The Preservation Press, 1983.

Parker, Freda. *Victorian Embroidery.* NY: Crescent Books, 1991.

Rankin, Chris. *Splendid Silk Ribbon Embroidery.* NY: Sterling Publishing Co., Inc., 1996.

Ruhling, Nancy and Freeman, John Crosby. *The Illustrated Encyclopedia of Victoriana, A Comprehensive Guide to the Designs, Customs, and Inventions of the Victorian Era.* Philadelphia PA, 1994.

Ryan, Mildred Graves. *The Complete Encyclopedia of Stitchery.* NY: Doubleday & Co., Inc., 1979.

Turpin-Delport, Lesley. *Satin and Silk Ribbon Embroidery.* South Africa: Triple T Publishing, 1993.

Walton, Perry. *The Story of Textiles.* 1925.

Weintraub, Stanley. *Victoria.* NY: Dutton, 1987.

Welch, Nancy. *Tassels: the Fanciful Embellishment.* Asheville, NC: Lark Books, 1992.

Wells, Jean. *Memorabilia Quilting.* CA: C&T Publishing, 1992.

Wilson, Erica. *Erica Wilson's Embroidery Book.* NY: Charles Scribner's Sons, 1973.

Wingate, Isabel B., and Mohler, June F. *Textile Fabrics and their Selection,* 8th Ed.

Sources

Silk Mori®, Silk Serica®, Japan
Gold and Silver, Metallic ribbons
and braids:
Kreinik Mfg. Co., Inc.
3106 Timanus Ln., Ste. 101
Baltimore, MD 21244
(800) 537-2166
www.kreinik.com

Silk Ribbons, Basting Thread:
YLI Corporation
161 W. Main St.
Rock Hill, SC 29730
(800) 296-8139
www.ylicorp.com

Waterlilies®, Soie Crystale®,
Impressions®:
The Caron Collection Ltd.
55 Old South Ave.
Stratford, CT 06615
(203) 381-9999

Hand-dyed Silk Perle and Spun
Silk Perle threads, Silk Chenille:
Victoria Clayton
6448 Freeman Rd.
Byron, NY 14422-9720
(716) 548-2620
www.hand-dyedfibers.com

Silk Dyes, Buttonhole Silk threads,
spooled silks:
Things Japanese
9805 N.E. 116th, Ste. 7160
Kirkland, WA 98034-4248
www.silkthings.com

Embroidery Threads:
Needle Necessities, Inc.
7211 Garden Grove Blvd. Stes.
B&C
Garden Grove, CA 92841
(714) 892-9211
www.needlenecessities.com

Paternayan® Persian Wool
Threads:
JCA, Inc.
35 Scales Ln.
Townsend, MA 01469
(978) 597-8794

Glass Seed Beads:
Shipwreck Beads
2500 Mottman Rd. SW
Olympia, WA 98512
(360) 754-2323
www.shipwreck-beads.com

The Crazy Quilt Society:
The Kirk Collection
1513 Military Ave.
Omaha, NE 68111
(800) 398-2542
www.kirkcollection.com
www.crazyquilt.com

Silk Fabrics:
Thai Silks
252 State St.
Los Altos, CA 94022
(800) 722-7455
www.thaisilks.com

Silk Fabrics & Dyes:
Rupert, Gibbon & Spider
P.O. Box 425
Healdsburg, CA 95448
(800) 442-0455
www.jacquardproducts.com

Foiling Supplies:
Laura Murray Designs
5021 15th Ave. S.
Minneapolis, MN 55417
(612) 825-1209
www.lauramurraydesigns.com

Crazy Quilting E-mail List:
www.quiltropolis.com

Buttons, leather, cotton laces, ribbons:
Home Sew
P.O. Box 4099
Bethlehem, PA 18018-0099
(800) 344-4739
www.homesew.com

Dyes, Marbling supplies:
Dharma Trading Co.
Box 150916
San Raphael, CA 94915
(800) 542-5227
www.dharmatrading.com

Index